P9-BYD-457

DUTY,
HONOR,
COUNTRY

DUTY, HONOR, COUNTRY

by

MICKEY HERSKOWITZ

Rutledge Hill Press™
Nashville, Tennessee

A Division of Thomas Nelson Publishers, Inc.
www.ThomasNelson.com

Copyright © 2003 by Mickey Herskowitz

All rights reserved. No portion of this book may be reproduced, stored in a retrieval system, or trans-mitted in any form or by any means—electronic, mechanical, photocopy, recording, or any other—except for brief quotations in printed reviews, without the prior permission of the publisher.

Published by Rutledge Hill Press, a Division of Thomas Nelson, Inc., P.O. Box 141000, Nashville, Tennessee 37214.

Photos on pages 2, 5, 7, 30, 31, 32, 35, 38, 45, 50, 51, 59, 69, 76, 77, 79, 80, 84, 85, 86, 89, 93, 96, 117, 131, 138, 143, 149, 150, 171, 182, 190, 200, 207 courtesy of the George H. W. Bush Presidential Library.
Photos on pages 41, 42, 43, 44, 60, 61, 66, 67, 208 courtesy of George H. W. Bush.
Photos on pages 46, 116, 118, 181, 184, 187, 203, 210, 211, 213 courtesy of the *Houston Chronicle*.
Photos on pages 159, 184 courtesy of the Houston Metropolitan Research Center, Houston Public Library.

Library of Congress Cataloging-in-Publication Data

Herskowitz, Mickey.
    Duty, honor, country : the life and legacy of Prescott Bush / by Mickey Herskowitz.
        p. cm.
    Includes bibliographical references and index.
    ISBN 1-4016-0009-3
    1. Bush, Prescott Sheldon, 1895-1972. 2. Bush, Prescott Sheldon, 1895-1972—Influence.
3. Legislators—United States—Biography. 4. United States. Congress. Senate—Biography. 5.
Bush family. 6. Bush, George, 1924- 7. Bush, George W. (George Walker), 1946- 8. Bush, Jeb.
I. Title.
E748.B8877 H47 2003
929.7'0973—dc21   2002153981

Printed in the United States of America

03 04 05 06 07—5 4 3 2 1

To Fathers and Sons . . .

Especially my own, starting with my dad, the gentlest man I have ever known, whose first and middle names, Herbert Sheldon, may have a familiar echo in the pages that follow.

To Steve and Brian, who have been a joy always, and the next generation, Garson and Max. And a special thought for Chris and Christian.

Contents

Foreword

$\mathcal{M}$y father was a remarkable man who not only believed in public service, but embodied the spirit of it.

He was a man in full: a patriot; a role model as a husband and father; a business leader, who created companies; and a scholar-athlete at Yale. He was a standout first baseman and a heavy hitter for the baseball team. He loved close harmony music and had a quartet until the day he died. He was the best golfer on campus and later in the Senate.

Dad played with some of the greatest golfers of his day, including Francis Ouimet and Bobby Jones, and he gained a special distinction as President Eisenhower's favorite partner.

He may have been the first candidate for the U. S. Senate who had members of the Yale Whiffenpoof Society sing at his rallies. This may not qualify as grass roots campaigning but music was a reward he gave the voters for listening to his speeches. When I led a seminar at Yale as part of the university's 300th anniversary, the longtime head of the Glee Club told me, "Your father was a legend here."

These are personal, not political thoughts. I always felt his career in the Senate was underrated. Yet his life was an inspiration to his sons and daughter, his grandchildren, and to those he served.

— GEORGE HERBERT WALKER BUSH

Acknowledgments

*F*irst, for his kindness and openness, I am hugely indebted to former President George Herbert Walker Bush. He allowed me access to documents and scrapbooks that were part of his private collection, and put me in touch with members of his exceptional family. For their cooperation and support, I thank Jean Becker, his chief of staff, and Linda Casey Popiel, another member of the former president's office.

Many curators and archivists rendered invaluable assistance: Mary Finch and Robert Holzweiss, of the George Bush Presidential Library at Texas A&M; and Betsy Pittman, of the Thomas J. Dodd Research Center at the University of Connecticut.

Janice Manuel was a meticulous copy editor. James Walden provided additional research. Two father-and-son teams were indispensable: Larry Stone, the creative publisher of Rutledge Hill Press, and Geoff Stone, a diligent and talented editor; and Bill Adler, whose fertile mind was never far from the project, and Bill Adler Jr., who surfed the Internet for us.

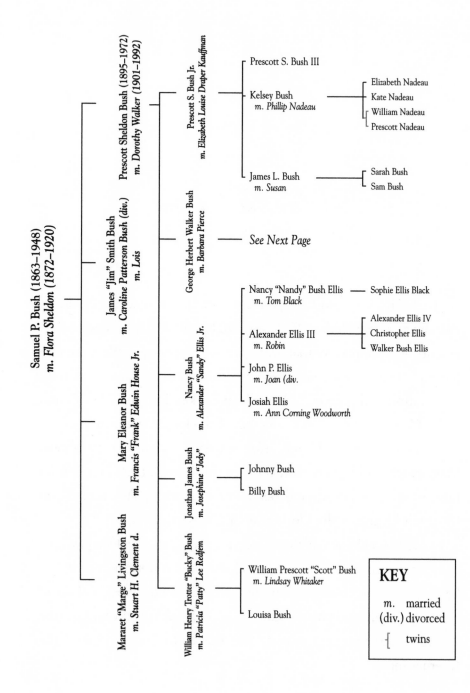

Samuel P. Bush (1863–1948)
m. Flora Sheldon (1872–1920)

James "Jim" Smith Bush
m. Caroline Patterson Bush (div.)
m. Lois

Prescott Sheldon Bush (1895–1972)
m. Dorothy Walker (1901–1992)

Prescott S. Bush Jr.
m. Elizabeth Louise Draper Kauffman

Prescott S. Bush III

Kelsey Bush
m. Phillip Nadeau

Elizabeth Nadeau
Kate Nadeau
William Nadeau
Prescott Nadeau

James L. Bush
m. Susan

Sarah Bush
Sam Bush

George Herbert Walker Bush
m. Barbara Pierce

See Next Page

Mary Eleanor Bush
m. Francis "Frank" Edwin House Jr.

Nancy Bush
m. Alexander "Sandy" Ellis Jr.

Nancy "Nandy" Bush Ellis
m. Tom Black

Sophie Ellis Black

Alexander Ellis III
m. Robin

Alexander Ellis IV
Christopher Ellis
Walker Bush Ellis

John P. Ellis
m. Joan (div.

Josiah Ellis
m. Ann Corning Woodworth

Jonathan James Bush
m. Josephine "Jody"

Johnny Bush
Billy Bush

Mararet "Marge" Livingston Bush
m. Stuart H. Clement d.

William Henry Trotter "Bucky" Bush
m. Patricia "Patty" Lee Redfern

William Prescott "Scott" Bush
m. Lindsay Whitaker

Louisa Bush

KEY

m.   married
(div.) divorced
{   twins

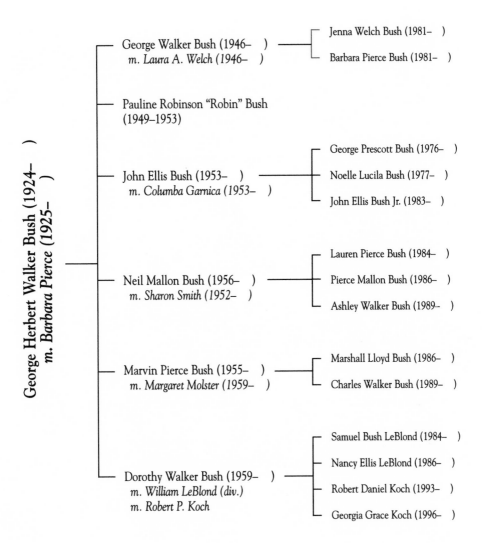

Introduction

There was a time when every boy or girl would be fed, along with his or her oatmeal, a great American myth: that any child can grow up to be president.

Recently two of them from the same family did just that. The son and grandson of a U. S. senator named Prescott Bush accomplished that goal only eight years apart. Another grandson has been twice elected the governor of Florida. This is quite a remarkable feat accomplished only once before by the Adamses, John and John Quincy, in the early 1800s.

The founder of the Bush political clan gained his wealth in a successful career in investment banking and gave back by serving in the government. He had the voice and distinguished looks of one born to perform, and the size and grace to excell in baseball and golf. His reputation in public life was close to pristine. He earned the respect of his colleagues and was adored by his four sons and a daughter and a host of grandkids.

For a man of these attainments, Prescott Bush seems ill treated, almost wildly underrated by historians, if they rated him at all. He served the state of Connecticut for ten years in the Senate, but his contributions were described by the media as hardly more than modest.

He did not chase rainbows, but he went to war, helped finance the radio and television giant CBS, co-sponsored the Peace Corps, funded the *Polaris* submarine, and was nearly always on the right side of the issues. He supported civil rights, a higher minimum wage, and the federal highway system. At the time, it should be noted, these were not necessarily popular stands.

He worked behind the scenes to make the Eisenhower presidency a success, and perhaps he did not receive more credit because he did such a good job of keeping the confidences that famous men entrusted to him. Although he accomplished quite a bit in his lifetime, it is what happened after his life that makes him most notable: the elections of George Herbert Walker Bush and George W. Bush to the White House. To produce stock of this quality takes courage, stamina, and most of all unwavering integrity.

He is now, if not before, a figure of historical importance. This book represents a search for Prescott Bush, who he was and what he stood for, the examples he set, the events he shared, and the lives he touched or influenced.

In the profiles or news accounts in which he sometimes appeared on the fringe, he came across as an exacting figure, old hat and a bit fussy. True, he was a formal man, who insisted that his grandchildren call him Senator. He wore coats and neckties to dinner, even at Kennebunkport on the coast of Maine, their summer retreat.

When his grandsons, Marvin and George W., showed up one

languid night in sweaty T-shirts and tennis shoes, they were ordered back to the guest cottage at the family compound and told to return in proper attire in five minutes. And he clocked them. Sprinting, they beat the deadline.

A New England moralist, although born in Ohio, he was not the kind of man one would describe as humble, but he found any kind of boasting intolerable. His insistence on being called Senator was not an act of vanity, but a lesson he sought to instill in the young ones in the kind of respect—they should have for those who served their country.

Politics was not discussed at his table. There were no pop quizzes. He didn't test them to see which grandchild could name the prime minister of Denmark. The talk tilted toward sports, music, and family matters. There were no arguments.

He must have been surprised when his son George decided to settle in Texas, and there launched his career in the barren, craggy earth of Midland, where only the oil rigs interrupted the monotony of the terrain. But he offered only encouragement. And he lived to see George W. follow the family path to Andover and Yale, but as a political newcomer he stressed his Texas roots not his Ivy League credentials.

In the 1950s Prescott and his dynamic Dorothy were frequent visitors to Midland. As a United States senator, he was treated as a celebrity. At six-foot-four, he was nearly always the most conspicuous figure in whatever room he entered.

When he came to Texas to campaign, however, it was on behalf of John Tower in his first race for the Senate seat vacated by Lyndon Johnson. He did not campaign for his son, nor was he asked. The code was established then and there. You could turn to your dad for advice, even a job referral or a campaign contribution. But you ran the race on your own. And you knew the race was not always to the swift or the strong, but that was the way to bet. You ran hard; you ran to win and you didn't whimper if you lost.

This was one of the lessons, handed down from Prescott, that every Bush family member accepted and honored. They were not clones, but three generations of political warriors indelibly linked. You could not picture his friends or associates giving Prescott a colorful nickname, as his boyhood chums did with George W., anointing him as the Bombastic Bushkin.

But each generation carried the torch, which is fitting. The grandfather was ice, the grandson fire, and the one in between, George Herbert Walker Bush, known as Poppy, had some of both.

DUTY,
HONOR,
COUNTRY

1

⎯⎯⎯∞⎯⎯⎯

Passing the Torch

They might have been the models for a recruiting poster. One was
a tall, handsome man in his mid-forties. The other, not yet out of his
teens, looked so boyish you had trouble picturing him behind the
wheel of a car, much less in the cockpit of a torpedo bomber.

It was early summer, but both wore suits and neckties as though
they were bound for a wedding, not sending the son off to war. They
walked halfway through the long lobby of New York's Pennsylvania
Station, down two flights of stairs, and followed the platform to the
track where the Atlantic Coast line would be taking the scenic route
to North Carolina.

There was only the slightest conversation between them, words
about letters and phone calls and Doing the Right Thing, as the older
man knew the younger one would. There was not much point in talking, anyway. All around them was the chaotic concert of a railroad station: the hiss of steam engines, hundreds of hurried footsteps, the
rumble of baggage carts, urgent shouts from families and train crews,

and more quietly but just as urgently, parents saying good-bye to their sons, and wives and girlfriends clinging to their own man in uniform.

Crowds of passengers pushed past couples locked in hungry embraces, eyes searching for the right track, the right train, the right car, dragging a suitcase or a large duffel bag. On his birthday, June 12, 1942, a week after he had graduated from Phillips Academy in Andover, George Herbert Walker Bush had traveled to Boston to be sworn in as a seaman second class in the United States Navy. Six months had passed since the Japanese bombed Pearl Harbor.

Now, on the sixth of August, Penn Station was an anthill of activity and George was leaving to report to the Naval Pre-Flight School in Chapel Hill, North Carolina, in the heart of Dixie.

He walked stride for stride beside his father, Prescott Bush, who at six feet four was two inches taller than his son, with a good overview of the milling throng. They stopped beside the train to Carolina and Prescott slipped an arm around George's

In 1941 Ensign George Bush, the navy's youngest pilot.

shoulder and hugged him, the movement a bit awkward for both, but holding it just long enough for each to feel the other's energy—and anxiety. George would not be wearing civilian clothes again for three years.

"I knew then how proud Dad was of me," George recalled years later. He discovered a new universe in the navy, and in North Carolina, but he wrote home of his delight in learning that another cadet in the aviation school was Ted Williams, the Boston Red Sox star outfielder. Ted had batted .406 in 1941, and no one could imagine then that this feat would not be matched for the next sixty years.

One year later, in June 1943, at the air base in Corpus Christi, Texas, Prescott Bush and his wife, Dorothy, watched their son receive his navy pilot's wings, and marked the occasion by giving him a pair of gold cuff links. Young George was now an ensign, and in another eight months he would be in the middle of the fighting, making bombing runs over the Pacific.

A point begs to be made here. There were politicians who served out of a sense of duty—we can give them that—but also with an awareness that a military record would be essential to run for office. Lyndon Johnson was a notable example, through his own admission; others were less open. But at eighteen, Ensign Bush did not see war as a stepping-stone. His history tells us so. He did not fantasize about being elected the Leader of the Free World.

When George's eldest son, George Walker Bush, was sworn in as governor of Texas in January 1995, the first George pressed into his son's hands the set of cuff links *his* father had given *him* when he went off to war. He had also written a letter, expressing his love and his pride, and his wife, Barbara, handed it to their son as they left the capitol to drive over to a prayer breakfast.

"I was preoccupied that morning," said George W. later. "At first,

I didn't think about the continuity, the grandfather part. The main thing I thought, the gift and the letter were from my dad. He was saying he was proud of me."

The morning was a busy one, with a host of family, friends, supporters, and media gathered for the inaugural events. At the prayer breakfast, George W. waved to the crowd before going inside the church to take his seat.

Once the service began, however, his thoughts returned to the gift and his father's letter. He pulled the letter out of his pocket and began rereading it. Just as the preacher got well started on his sermon, tears began to stream down the new governor's face. The rest of the congregation may have thought the preacher was really on his game, but that wasn't what had moved George W. He later described the moment:

> I was able to compose myself and gave my speech, but I was deeply touched. We do express our love and I think it's understood, as well, that we can be both weepers and laughers.
>
> What got me was the last line of the letter. It said, Now it's your turn.

Indeed, the cuff links had been no casual gift. They were not just some favorite bit of family memorabilia passed from one generation to the next like baseball cards (although his generation would have done cartwheels over a really fine collection of baseball cards). This was a symbolic passing of the torch, a possession that represented war and peace and the keeping of the family faith.

Across the years, from hand to hand to hand, destiny reached out to them. Prescott Sheldon Bush carried the flame first. He was a contradiction in terms, a modest politician who strived to remain discreet and trustworthy. If he did not always succeed, he came closer than most.

The late Connecticut senator is today a more prominent figure of history, retroactively highlighted by the astounding achievements of his son George and his grandson George W., who became the forty-first and forty-third presidents of the United States, and his grandson Jeb, who became governor of Florida.

It is important to place Prescott Bush, who he was and what he begat, in the context of his political times, the 1950s. This was a decade that creased the century, so that one could almost fold it and pop it into an envelope.

We think of the fifties as our last decade of national innocence before the sexual revolution, in which there were darned few draft dodgers. Then

Prescott Bush and his American-made car; he never bought a foreign model.

came television as teacher and baby-sitter; space shots, satellites, computers, cell phones and the wiring of the world, giving us the voracious Internet, where one can read such "wisdom" as this: Never judge another man unless you have walked a mile in his shoes.

Then, if he gets mad, you are a mile away and he is barefooted. The second half of this wisdom was totally contrary to the values of Prescott Bush and his descendants. He was almost too nice to be in politics, which is why the family prefers to think of this profession as public service.

Prescott was largely overlooked, ignored, or forgotten by the people who wrote the history of his times. Scholars tended to describe him as well liked, widely admired, but a man who did not leave much of an imprint in the way of major legislation or an impact on government. His relatives, political and blood, disagree.

"He was a coauthor of the bills that created the national highway system, and John F. Kennedy's Peace Corps," says his first of four sons, Prescott Bush Jr. "He supported the civil rights movement and spoke out against the tactics of Joe McCarthy, when those were not popular stands."

In fact, Prescott was the quiet actor behind the scenes who whispered the lines that led to McCarthy, at long last, being dragged off the stage. Yet if not for events that occurred many years after his death, he might have been lost altogether as an example of moral rightness and unflinching honesty.

"When he retired from the Senate," recalls Barbara Bush, the wife of one president and mother of another, "Prescott sat at his desk and wrote checks to return every dime of the campaign money that had been raised. Every dime! What had been spent, he made up for out of his own pocket.

"But he returned it all, addressed the envelopes and put them in the mail. How many times have you heard of a politician doing such a thing? I haven't. He set an example for everybody."

For himself, he established rigid standards of grace and scruples. He was more than considerate or tolerant. In an old-fashioned sense, he remained throughout his life a man of chivalry.

He was Prescott Sheldon Bush, once content to be the moderator of the Town Hall in Greenwich, later thrilled to be a senator, whose progeny broke all previous records. He became the father of a president, who in turn became the father of a president and two governors.

Barbara, four-year-old George W., and Poppy greet Dorothy and Prescott at the Midland airport in 1950.

The line that began in the United States Senate would later include two governors, of Texas and Florida, and two presidents, which adds up to a family that eclipsed all others. Prescott and his heirs outscored the Kennedys with their boundless potential.

Spreading out from their quiet, reserved New England roots, the Bushes moved beyond the Roosevelts; the Tafts; the Rockefellers; the Longs of Louisiana, who behaved as if they were running an empire, not a state; and even the Adamses, John and John Quincy.

It is a pretty remarkable thing to elect a father and son to the presidency. Yet it happened just eight years apart. This convergence has occurred only once before, with the Adamses, in the infancy of the Republic and twenty-four years apart.

John Adams followed George Washington into office, in 1801, and died on July 4, 1826, the same day as Thomas Jefferson and less than six months after his son's inauguration as the nation's sixth president. The last words of John Adams were wistful and wrong: "Jefferson survives."

This is as far as we can climb on this particular slope without using the *D* and *L* words. To both George Bushes, the very sounds of *dynasty* and *legacy* are like the scrapings of chalk on a blackboard.

"We can talk about my dad having a legacy, and that's all right," said George Herbert Walker Bush, "because it's out there. But I don't have a legacy, and I'm pretty sure George doesn't think he has one. Maybe a hundred years from now, the people who care about such things can look it up and draw their conclusions. Not in my lifetime."

If you want a short conversation with George the First, mention the Bush dynasty. "We don't think that way," he says repeatedly, and you get the sense he is stifling a scream. "We have nothing to pass on except our willingness to serve. We are not about exercising power. None of us thought getting elected to high office was our destiny. There was no political talk around the dinner table. Our family believed in giving back to the community. My dad did that with his Town Meetings. It started there."

Left unasked is the question: If this is a dynasty, why did the voters take away his job and give it to Bill Clinton in 1992? One can talk about the economy and grocery scanners and the third-party candidacy of Ross Perot, but the question continues to be an open wound. When George W. Bush emerged as the runaway favorite for the Republican nomination in 2000, an early poll showed that 40 percent of the respondents thought they were supporting the architect of the war in the Persian Gulf—his father.

So we are required to return to Prescott Bush and the concept of noblesse oblige, persons of privilege behaving nobly, serving unselfishly for the greater good of humanity.

"He demanded very high morals of his family," says William Trotter Bush, known as Bucky, the youngest of the four brothers. "You go down the Ten Commandments. He lived that."

If any of his sons were asked to describe their father, the first response would be: "Big man. Usually the tallest man in any room he walked into; very strong, a really big man." In his mid-thirties, Prescott Bush was six-foot-four and weighed 250 with no flab. He had filled out from the gangly first baseman of his Yale days, and his voice was rich and deep, a train rumbling out of a tunnel. Everything about him spoke of command. He seemed to his young sons and daughter a giant whose presence filled the three-story, eight-bedroom home on Grove Lane.

They were well-behaved kids and to a degree fear motivated their behavior, but it was the fear of failing to live up to his expectations. It didn't happen often, four or five times, but when Prescott Jr. or George, or both, were guilty of mischief, all Dorothy Bush needed to say was, "Your father will hear about this when he gets home," to work them into a state of trembling anxiety. The punishment was never as bad as they feared, but the waiting was.

And yet, Prescott had a tender side that could lift a person's spirit almost without their being aware. When Robin, the beautiful, blonde three-year-old daughter of George and Barbara was dying of leukemia at Sloan-Kettering Hospital in New York, Prescott asked the exhausted, heartsick Barbara to spend a Sunday at the house in Greenwich.

He asked if she would mind going with him to visit the plot he had picked where he would be buried at the historic Putnam Cemetery. He wanted her opinion. In bright sunshine that afternoon, the two of them walked up a gentle hillside lush with trees. His hand cupped her elbow, a touch that was like an embrace.

He had picked out a tranquil spot, with a freshly planted lilac bush and a dogwood tree on either side of a modest headstone that would say, simply, BUSH—three feet high and four feet wide. He pointed to an imposing mausoleum nearby and said, "I knew old so-and-so. Thought a lot of himself, didn't he, Bar."

Barbara felt a calm and a peacefulness she had not known since before the day eight months earlier when she and George had become alarmed by their little girl's lethargy. And then she understood that her father-in-law had shown her the place little Robin would be laid to rest.

His passions defined Prescott Bush and they were (not always in this order, but close): his family, his country, his faith, the Senate, Yale, golf, music, and baseball. He would never have claimed that he led an all-American life, yet no phrase better describes it. He was not obsessed with winning; he simply had little tolerance for losing.

On those occasions when he and his wife played bridge with

another couple, Prescott sometimes would be withdrawn or impatient. "He doesn't like 'visiting bridge,'" Dorothy explained. "He wants to bid and win and skip the talk."

Yet in his student days, in business and in the Senate, even in his idle moments, Prescott was a peacemaker. Early in his first year in Washington, as he was riding through a tough neighborhood near Griffith Stadium, home of the city's baseball team, he ordered his aide to stop the car so he could jump out and break up a fight between two teenagers. He pulled the larger one off a much smaller lad. Looking up, and up, at this towering figure, both boys obediently scrambled to their feet.

The fight was about one of them taking back whatever had been said about the other's girlfriend. Before he left, Prescott told the larger of the two, "This is no way to settle an argument. You don't pick on people smaller than you." Turning to the shorter one, he added, "And you need to work on blocking a punch."

Each of his children idolized him, which is what one expects of children, none more so than the second son. Minutes after his swearing-in ceremonies, January 1988, the first conscious thought of George Bush was: "I wonder what the old man would think of his boy now?"

George Herbert Walker Bush is sworn in as the 41st president by Chief Justice Rehnquist (back to camera); Barbara (far right) barely made the picture.

11

Prescott Bush formed his sense of duty early and passed it on to his sons, most famously to George, who passed it to his own children. In 1916 Prescott was one of two Yale seniors to volunteer for active duty with the Tenth Regiment of the Connecticut National Guard, when he heard the unit might be headed for the Mexican border and the pursuit of the marauding Pancho Villa. The mission to Mexico did not develop, but a year later Captain Bush, of the 158th Artillery Battalion, served in the trenches in France under General John J. Pershing.

To this day George Herbert Walker Bush—a Phi Beta Kappa at Yale, decorated navy pilot, congressman, ambassador to the United Nations, envoy to China, vice president and president— would not presume to think he was the man his father was. It is startling to realize there is nothing artificial about this sentiment. He means it.

The fondness of the Bush family for repeating their names leads to an abundance of Prescotts, Walkers, Sheldons, and Georges, providing endless hours of fun and confusion for the media. The Bush insiders have coped with part of the identity crisis by instituting a code, referring to the two presidents as Number 41 and Number 43.

Months before George W. won his extra-inning, roller-coaster race against Al Gore, Andrew Sullivan, a British expatriate, speculated in the *New York Times* magazine on the implications of a Bush restoration: "What are the odds . . . that one living president could be directly related to another living one? About the same as the likelihood of a meteorite hitting the White House. . . .

"My own homeland, Britain, has a monarchy and a peerage system where heredity is destiny. But no British prime minister has ever been elected whose ancestor also held the office. . . .

"Sure, a certain amount of nepotism has always been a feature of American life . . . yet, we seem almost sanguine about the fact that the members of our political leadership are increasingly related to one another."

The Brit compared the 2000 election to a War of the Roses, "between the son of Albert Gore Sr., southern populist, and the grandson of Prescott Bush, bleeding heart Republican."

So it seems fair to ask: What hath Prescott wrought? Where do such families, such people, who overcame huge odds and untold cynics to achieve the highest office in the land, come from?

"Shocked?" repeats Prescott Bush Jr. with an echo. "I don't think my father would be shocked that his son and grandson became president. I think he would be ecstatic and very, very proud."

Prescott did not live to see either of these triumphs, of course, but his influence was surely felt. He gave his children Andover, Yale, and an abiding love of sports and competition. Of more direct value, he instilled in them a moral justification for being successful and doing more with money than counting it. You only need to hear the voice of George and see the way his face shines when he talks about his father to appreciate the phrase "hero worship."

"I thought it was rather flattering," he says, "when Tom Brokaw put a little thing about me in his book *The Greatest Generation*. I don't think of it that way. It was simply doing your duty, and I got that from my dad, not just in war, in what you put back into society.

"I would say his generation was a contender for that title. Their war didn't have the same dimension to it. It mainly involved Europe.

13

But a great wave of patriotism swept the country, and the young men of his time rushed off to serve in that war. Then they came home and started building the great industries of this country, and to set a tone, politically.

"Dad didn't have the national prominence of some of his colleagues. Didn't seek it. He didn't have a personal agenda. He wasn't goal-oriented like his son. He wasn't a media darling. He was more the prototype of the distinguished senator. He looked the part and he acted the part."

2

⟨⟩

Faith of His Fathers

Prescott Bush was a circumspect man who believed that decent people did not talk openly or loosely, even in private, about religion, money, or sex.

In the 1990s in Washington, D.C., the third topic may have soared to the top of the charts. But in his era Prescott found himself walking a fine line to keep his faith, which was strong and deep-seated, out of politics. His son George had a firm and sincere religious base, but was never comfortable taking it public.

George W., once the wild seed of the family, was the Bush most at ease with his expression of faith, the one who spoke of reading a passage from the Bible each night and was embraced by the evangelical wing of his party. "He's our family Bible expert," confirmed his mother, Barbara.

The family did not discover religion in the year 2000, of course. It was there all along, more than a century of commitment. Honorable people come from honorable roots, which brings us to some little-known family history.

A note, written on the letterhead of George Bush and dated August 21, 2001, says:

Dear Mr. President,

I thought you might like to know more about your heritage, thus this little story about your great-great-grandfather—who was the father of Samuel Prescott Bush, my dad's dad.

Is this clear?

Devotedly,
Dad

The note refers to a memoir written by a Bush family friend, William Barrett, and privately printed in 1907. What follows is drawn and condensed from that essay.

The story of the Bush men—indeed, the whole Bush inheritance—really begins almost two hundred years ago, with one Obediah Bush, who at age fifteen headed west to do his duty and seek his fortune.

During the War of 1812, young Obediah left his native Vermont with "a number of other boys" to help garrison a fort at Buffalo, New York. Once his military service was over, he became a schoolmaster in his new home state, eventually marrying a former student, the winsome Miss Harriet Smith. The newlyweds settled in Rochester, New York, where they were among the earliest residents, and Obediah opened a general store. The store prospered, and Obediah and Harriet began a family, eventually having seven children.

In 1848 gold was discovered at Sutter's Mill, out in California, and like so many others across the country, Obediah came down with gold fever, drawn by the bewitching promises of the glittering mineral. Within a year, he left behind his family and headed west, one of the original forty-niners.

Despite the rigors of gold country, where many men met only disappointment or even a violent end, Obediah's experience seems to have been fairly positive, even if he did not become fabulously rich. In fact, he liked that part of the country so well that he soon decided it was where he would like to settle permanently. In 1851 he started east by sea to retrieve his wife and seven children and bring them west.

This was no small undertaking. The voyage was a long, dangerous trip that required sailing far to the south in order to pass all the way around South America before heading north again, toward an eastern seaport.

Unfortunately Obediah never reached home; he died on the voyage and was buried at sea. Fulfillment of this Bush pioneer's dream would have to wait for later generations, when it would eventually take shape in ways he could not have imagined.

James Smith Bush was Obediah's eldest son, the second child of the seven. He was born in Rochester on June 15, 1825. James, by all descriptions, was a puny and sickly child, with a fragile build and weak lungs. His mother hardly expected to rear him. A cousin, Dr. A. G. Smith, a blunt and outspoken physician, looked at the infant and told his mother, "You better knock him in the head, for if he lives he will never amount to anything."

His mother had little reason to expect this child would ever survive, but she did not give up so easily. Over time, nurtured tenderly by his mother and no doubt aided by his own passion for exercise, James not only survived but grew stronger and healthier each year. He received his first formal education at a private institution called simply the High School, and patterned after the English Lancastrian system.

At sixteen he went away to Yale College in New Haven, Connecticut, where he was able to begin as a sophomore. Though he could not know it at the time, he began a Bush family tradition that would continue for at least four more generations. "His classmates speak of him as tall and slender in person, rather grave of mien, except when engaged in earnest conversation or good-humored repartee; ever kind and considerate and always a gentleman—still, very strong in his likes and dislikes. He made many friends. Anxious to make the most of his opportunities, he ranked high in his studies. Fond of athletics, he achieved considerable reputation as an oarsman, rowing stroke in his class crew. He was also quite noted as a high jumper," wrote William Barrett.

[Does anything jump out at us here? Tall and slender; ranked high in his studies (George the First). Good-humored repartee; strong in his likes and dislikes (George W.). Made many friends (a common trait to all the Bush men).]

James Smith Bush had set the bar for those to come, literally. He had started college with the intention of becoming a Presbyterian minister. But with his father off panning for gold, the family needed his financial help, so he decided to study law. After his admission to the bar, he opened an office in Rochester, taking as a partner a young lawyer named Root and creating a firm called Root and Bush. This led to several terrible puns, such as: A Bush could hardly be expected to flourish without a Root.

In October 1851, the year of his father's death at sea, James married Sarah, the daughter of Dr. Samuel Freeman, of Saratoga Springs. She was known as the town beauty, and they met when he passed her on the street, spun around and introduced himself. He took his young bride to Rochester, but their happiness was of short duration. She was stricken with a fever of the brain and died, only eighteen months after the wedding.

Her husband's grief was so deep, and he was so beyond consoling that he could never again speak of her without emotion. Her death marked a new direction in his life as his thoughts were turned to things eternal. He had become interested in the Episcopal church through his wife, and he resolved to give up the law and prepare himself for the ministry.

In time he was ordained by Horatio Potter, the bishop of New York, and at once took charge of a new parish at Orange, New Jersey, remaining there for ten years. During the Civil War, Bush was a staunch Union man and insisted on having the Stars and Stripes flung to the breeze from the church tower, over strenuous objections from some of his congregation who possessed Southern sympathies.

During his pastorate in Orange, he had a second chance at love and married Harriet Eleanor Fay. A native of Concord, Massachusetts, she was the daughter of Samuel Howard Fay and a relative of Samuel Prescott, who rode with Paul Revere during the Revolutionary War.

James Russell Lowell said of her, "She possessed the finest mind and was the most brilliant young woman of my day."

Up to now, James Bush had led a mundane existence: As a baby his survival had been in doubt. He excelled at Yale, endured the deaths of his father and his first wife, and switched from the law to the ministry. In 1865 he accepted an invitation from Commodore Rogers to accompany him on a cruise aboard the *Vanderbilt*, as secretary and acting chaplain. The object of this expedition was to show that the monitors could safely sail the broad ocean, as they had been considered in general fit for only harbor defense.

The fleet consisted of the flagship *Vanderbilt*, the monitor *Monadnock*, the *Powhatan*, and the *Tuscarora*. They set sail for South America, stopping at the principal ports, reaching San Francisco and then returning home. The trip delighted Bush, providing excitement and unexpected occurrences. He wrote a paper, "The Trip of the *Monadnock*," which he read before the Concord Lyceum in 1886 and in lectures around the state.

Illustrating his tendency to introduce a moral and spiritual side, he related an incident on board the ship under the charge of Lieutenant Commander Franklin: "A fire had been discovered in dangerous proximity to the magazine. The danger of explosion was imminent, and the men rushed forward in great consternation. Not one was found daring enough to obey the order to go below and extinguish the fire.

"Seizing the hose in his own hands, Franklin leaped into the hold. One of the gunners followed him, exclaiming, 'Mr. Franklin, you're a brave man, you shan't go to hell alone.' The fire was put out."

Characteristically, James Bush would add after a pause, "Is it not by the courage always to do the right thing that the fires of hell shall be put out?" "Do the Right Thing" became a Bush mantra, along with "Give Credit to Others" and "Be Loyal" and "Always, Always Play Fair."

While cruising along the West Indies, a French prisoner who had swum out to the ship was returned to his jailers and shot. Bush wrote, "Let us hope that the prayers said over his dead body were heard by the good Father above, and that in the divine justice and mercy his soul has found a refuge from the cruel severity of which he was the victim here."

Having compassion for lesser fortunate souls is a trait that would be passed on from James to Samuel to Prescott and on and on.

In San Francisco James met with and was entertained by Governor Henry Haight, a friend and Yale classmate, one of the men for whom the Haight-Ashbury District was named. James received a call to the Grace Church in San Francisco, and he stayed as its minister for five years. In 1871 he accepted a call to the Church of the Ascension, across the continent at West Brighton, Staten Island, which was to be his last regular assignment.

His nearness to New York brought him into friendship with many ministers, and especially with Heber Newton, who had just written a book that created a great disturbance in the church. In 1883 James published a book entitled *More Words about the Bible*, which he dedicated to Newton. A year later James resigned, largely because of a change of religious belief.

George William Curtis said of James Bush, "He was so transparent . . . that the slow change in his religious view was felt by his congregation before it was comprehended. He was never dogmatic or formal, and his mind was so truthful, his spirit so reverent, and his feeling so refined, that there was no iconoclastic strain or sentiment in his expression.

"By the larger part of the society he was greatly beloved, and in his community he was universally respected. His sincerity and wholesome humor and kindly temper prevented the least morbid feeling during the deep emotion which accompanied his separation from his church."

Years earlier, as the guest of Curtis at his home in Ashfield, Bush confided that while the traditions of his church and its personal association were very precious to him, its creed satisfied him no longer.

"One day, I quoted the first lines of Emerson's 'Problem,'" said curtis, "and [James] said to me, with almost startling earnestness, 'What is that?'

"It appeared that he had never seen the poem, and I immediately took it down and read it to him. I never had such a rapt auditor, and with great feeling he said, as I ended, 'Why, why, that is my faith.'"

A Dr. Stebbins of San Francisco wrote: "I discovered early in my acquaintance with Mr. Bush that his theological garments were outgrown. Although I was not familiar with him, we met often enough to get the flavor of each other's mind, and to raise the question with me, 'Where will he come out?' He was by nature and constitution a Liberal, but did not know it, until his own moral nature had grown strong enough to break the shell of automatic habit."

James Bush moved to Concord in 1884. He was drawn there because it was the home of his wife's ancestors and had excellent schools. During his five years' residence, he thoroughly identified himself with the town and its people. He became an enthusiastic lover of Concord, an admirer of its river and ponds, its woods and valleys. He was wont to take long walks, as he said, to "drink in the beauties of nature." His face and form were familiar to everybody in the town, both young and old, and to meet him and receive his warm and courtly greeting was a bright spot in the day. For some time he preached at the chapel at South Lincoln, always walking to and fro if the weather was good.

James fully expected to end his days in Concord, but circumstances made it advisable for him to go to Ithaca, New York. His youngest son was to enter Cornell University, and it was thought best for the family to take up residence there, at least for the time being. With tears in his eyes he told his friends good-bye and departed, never again to return. He left Concord in May 1889, and moved his family to Ithaca, into a house he had purchased on Buffalo Hill.

After his death, the Reverend Mr. Day, then of Ithaca, wrote: "He gained a position in the public respect and affection that few men could have won in years." There were intimations, unknown to any but his family, that though the spirit was growing in vigor, the body was failing. Any exertion tired him, he complained of shortness of breath, and on November 11, 1889, he had a severe heart attack and in a few hours had passed away, at the age of sixty-four years and five months. He was buried at Ithaca. His widow and four children survived him. Freeman, the oldest, graduated from Columbia and was ranching in Colorado. Samuel Prescott Bush, a graduate of Stevens College, majored in mechanical engineering. Harold earned an engineering degree from Cornell. And Eleanor Howe Bush was a student at Smith College.

Samuel appeared to have been the family star, and his athletic and musical interests would reappear in his descendants. He was a vice president of the student body at Stevens in his sophomore year, and competed on both the baseball and tennis teams. He sang baritone in one glee club and first bass in another. His son Prescott would inherit his vocal talents, which would spread to the next generation through four of Prescott's five children: Jonathan, Prescott Jr., Bucky, and Nancy. George claims that he is the only one who didn't inherit the ability to sing.

After his graduation Samuel moved to Columbus, Ohio, and went to work for the Pennsylvania Railroad. In 1894, he married the twenty-two-year-old Flora Sheldon, the daughter of a dry goods merchant and bank officer. The Bush family bloodline was instantly enriched. One of her ancestors was the first Robert R. Livingston, the Puritan dissenter who left Scotland after the Stuart restoration and made his way to America in 1673.

A Democrat in Ohio politics, Samuel was a pivotal influence, active in ways that would inspire Prescott. Samuel ran a railroad in Milwaukee, then returned to Columbus to serve as president of a company that manufactured railway equipment.

He was a force in the Ohio Chamber of Commerce and made at least two major contributions to the American efforts in World War I. He organized the first war chest drive and at the request of Bernard Baruch served in Washington with the War Industries Board. His granddaughter Nancy Bush described him as "a high-minded, impressive, wonderful-looking person." Along the way, he founded a golf course in Ohio that became the first training ground for Jack Nicklaus.

Politics, public service, golf—in each generation were planted the seeds of the next. For their faith and perseverance and public spirit, James Smith Bush was clearly the founding father.

"In stature," William Barrett's story concluded, "Mr. Bush was above the average, about six feet, rather slender in build, of graceful carriage. He had a fine, strong, handsome face, with a kindly smile and charming grace of manner. His chief characteristics, it seems to me, were a nature free from guile, and a gentle cordiality of manner refreshing to see. Pure and unspotted from the world, he was in the truest sense a spiritually minded man. Possessing strong opinions, he never was offensive or aggressive in asserting them. . . ."

This, then, was James Smith Bush, the grandfather of George Herbert Walker Bush.

3

God and Man at Yale

For most of his years Prescott Bush led a charmed life. Born on May 15, 1895, the son of Samuel Prescott and Flora Sheldon Bush, he attended the Douglas Elementary School, at the time the *only* school in Columbus, Ohio.

Later he would look on his early education as an ecumenical time. His classmates were of all nationalities—Irish, Italian, German, and African-American. He would say, proudly, "I always felt that [experience] gave me a sense of balance about ethnic problems that I found useful in later life, particularly in political life."

After Prescott finished the eighth grade, his parents decided he needed some prep school polish, and he was sent east to Saint George's, an Episcopalian school in Rhode Island. Even though his public school experience had been positive, Prescott appreciated the benefits he enjoyed at St. George's—perhaps more than most of the 125 boys, since he had more to contrast it with. The school boasted an athletic field and a gymnasium, and Prescott made the most of them, starring in football, baseball, and basketball. He was also active in both the drama and civics club. The latter was a debating society, taking up such issues of the moment as, "How do we feel about a protective tariff versus a tariff for revenue only?"

While Prescott was at Saint George's, he considered following in his grandfather's footsteps and preparing for the ministry. He had made no commitment, however, "to my family or myself," when he qualified for Yale, already highly rated as a scholar and a sportsman.

As James Smith Bush before him, and others to follow, Prescott arrived in New Haven in the fall of 1914, a member of the Class of '17. Yale was founded in 1701 by one Abraham Pierson, its first rector, making it the third oldest university in the United States. Known at the time as the Collegiate School, it at first met in the rector's home. The school moved to New Haven in 1716 with the assistance of Elihu Yale, a merchant who contributed to the cause nine bales of goods, 417 books, and a portrait and the coat of arms of King George I.

In 1718 the school's name was changed in honor of this benefactor. The school has sometimes been called "Old Eli," in memory of the same connection, and a student has often been referred to as an "Eli."

One might also note that Yale was Big Blue before IBM owned its first chip. The brand of football played in the Ivy League was still considered respectable, certainly in the East. Yale had won a national championship as recently as 1909.

In normal times, whatever those are, Prescott would have sailed through his undergraduate studies and gone on to law school. But these were not just any times. During Prescott's junior year, the papers were filled with reports of trouble on the Mexican border.

Mexico had suffered a long period of revolution, then virtual civil war. In 1916 Poncho Villa tried to instigate conflict between the United States and the Mexican government, which he didn't like, by invading the U.S. territory. On January 9 he and his men killed seventeen miners in New Mexico; on March 9 another seventeen Americans died when Villa raided Columbus, New Mexico. In response U.S. General John J. "Black Jack" Pershing led a punitive expeditionary force of twelve thousand troops deep into northern Mexico, where they stayed, despite attack by Mexican federal forces, until February 1917.

Joining other young men who were concerned about their country's welfare and wanting to do their duty (and perhaps pursue adventure), Prescott joined the National Guard. This sense of service and duty is a trait Prescott would pass on to his sons and grandsons. In June he was called up for active duty. The so-called Yale Battalion, composed of four batteries of field artillery, and two others from Connecticut made it as far as Tobyhanna, Pennsylvania. There they trained under regular army officers for most of the summer before being discharged in time to return to school for September classes.

Reflecting on this period of his life from the distance of the late 1960s, Prescott said that his father wasn't able "to support me. He had a modest income, but he couldn't support his adult children, and I didn't want him to, anyway."

This may be how he remembered the circumstances, or may simply be the gentle shadings of time, making the roads more narrow, the turns sharper, the forks more sudden. But the record seems clear that the family lived well, and Samuel P. Bush put a heavy stock on self-reliance. More likely he was unwilling, rather than unable, to provide for his adult children, especially the ones who graduated from Yale.

Yale's star first baseman and power hitter was lanky Prescott Bush, sitting third from the right in the middle row.

Along with his academic brilliance, Prescott was successful on the field. He was not only a slugging first basemen for the Yale Bulldogs, but was the golfer they called on for the toughest matches. He sang in the Glee Club as a member of the Whiffenpoofs—he probably had the best voice of any first baseman ever to represent Yale. Years later he would be voted to their all-time quartet.

Founded in 1909 as part of the Yale Glee Club, it was originally known as the varsity quartet. Since winters in New Haven were not ideal for outdoor vocalizing, the group began to meet one night a week at Mory's, where a man named Louis Linder operated what was called the Dear Old Temple Bar.

They ate, drank, and made music, and their numbers expanded. The

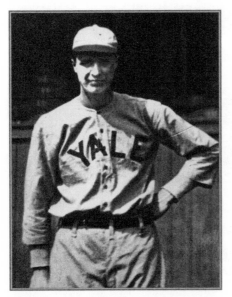

Poppy Bush followed his dad's footsteps, literally, playing first base and twice leading Yale to national college finals.

Whiffenpoof name was taken from a character in a Victor Herbert musical comedy. The lyrics for the Whiffenpoof Song were adapted from an unpublished version of Kipling's poem "Gentlemen-Rankers."

It was with some embarrassment that the group learned in 1959 the music had been composed by a Harvard man, Guy H. Scull, Class of 1899. Nevertheless, the show went on and does to this day.

The love of "America's" game caused a tidal wave in the family gene pool. Big George went on to play for Yale and captain his team.

A passion for the game would be passed on to each of the grandsons. But it was George W. who earned their envy, not as a player but as one of the owners of the Texas Rangers.

During his senior year at Yale, Prescott Bush began to consider that he might someday run for public office, and decided he would enter law school. Also that year, he was tapped for membership in Skull and Bones, a society into which both George and George W. also would be invited.

According to early sources, Skull and Bones was founded by a group that broke away from Phi Beta Kappa, which had ended its own bonds of secrecy. A picture of a skull and crossbones adorned

Prescott, at right, was voted one of the all-time Yale close harmony singers.

the door of the chapel where they met, and this became their symbol. The nineteenth-century Gothic structure stood near the center
of the Yale campus, at one end of High Street. The building became
known as the Tomb, adding to the macabre image.

In time two giant padlocks and an electronic security system were
added to discourage unwanted visitors.

Only fifteen new members, always seniors, are tapped each year.
This way, in theory, they will have left the university before being
tempted to talk of their experiences. But Bonesmen are everywhere
in the American establishment: in Congress, the CIA, the courts,
Wall Street, and the media. Their numbers have included President
William Howard Taft; Henry Luce, founder of the Time-Life empire;
the financier Dean Witter; and numerous judges, ambassadors, senators, and university presidents. Among these are Senator John
Kerry of Massachusetts; David Boren, the president of the University

of Oklahoma; and William F. Buckley Jr., the writer and intellectual whose book *God and Man at Yale* became a conservative manifesto. And, of course, the list includes a long line of Bushes and Walkers. A painting five feet high of George Herbert Walker Bush was hung on a wall in the Tomb in 2000, taking its place among portraits of the club's most conspicuous successes.

Membership has provided many with a network that would be valuable to their futures, which fueled the many conspiracy theories. In 1992 Skull and Bones became one of the last two secret societies to admit women.

In a 1968 yearbook parody, Lanny Davis (Class of '67, one year before George W., and later special counsel in the Clinton administration) described an ideal, mythical group. The mix would consist of a football captain, a conspicuous radical, a Whiffenpoof, a swimming captain, a notorious drunk with a ninety-four average, a filmmaker, a political columnist, a religious leader, a chairman of the Lit, a foreigner, a ladies' man with two motorcycles, an ex-serviceman, an African-American—if there were enough to go around—and a guy nobody else in the group had heard of, ever.

For years the society possessed a skull that members called Geronimo, purported to be that of the Apache chief. Prescott Bush himself was rumored to be part of the raiding party that made off with this treasured artifact from the archaeology building.

The escapade reminds one of the three defenses offered by the lawyer for a client whose dog had been accused of biting a neighbor: (1) My dog did not bite that man; (2) if he did, my dog was provoked; and (3) I don't have a dog.

There is a story told about Prescott Bush, perhaps the only one on record to reveal a brash and playful side. In his defense, there are three arguments: (1) Nobody knows for certain that he stole the skull of Geronimo, the great Apache chief, as a fraternity prank at Yale; (2) if he did, he acted with others, not alone; and (3) forensic evidence later proved the skull was not Geronimo's.

In the 1980s Ned Anderson, a former Apache tribal chairman in Arizona, pressured the society to produce the skull in question. Tests and measurements then showed that the skull did not match Anderson's records, and it was duly returned to the Tomb.

Anderson did not give up, however. He referred the matter to his congressman, John McCain. McCain in turn tried to arrange a meeting between the Apache spokesman and George Bush, then the vice president. Given the facts that his father had been vindicated, the skull was apparently not that of Geronimo, and no evidence existed of a theft, Bush politely declined to take the meeting, and the case was dropped.

The Bonesmen still refer to the skull, however, as "Geronimo."

Some of the alleged Skull and Bones traditions have been dismissed, as well. The standard answer to the claim that each member received a graduation gift of fifteen thousand dollars is, "I haven't seen mine." As for the initiation-night ritual of branding new members on the buttocks, Lanny Davis revealed the trick: The initiate was shown the brand, blindfolded, and then touched with the tip of a hot match. Given the power of suggestion, some were certain they had felt the sensation of a branding, at least a temporary one.

Gone are the days of members reciting a personal sexual history, a practice that may have helped to tighten the bonds of the Bonesmen, but could hardly have thrilled their girlfriends. Also discontinued was

Among his many athletic talents, Prescott Bush was a starter on the Bulldogs' hockey team.

the "Mirror Images" night, when each society member was frankly and brutally evaluated by the others. These have been replaced by biographies and by Sunday and Thursday after-dinner discussions that may range from funny to cerebral.

Many older members, the "patriarchs," lamented the passing of the tougher traditions. They say the male bonding and the rituals were inseparable from an almost missionary vision of public service, a certainty that a cadre of elite Yale men could reshape the globe.

The secrecy concealed the fact that the club has high and daunting goals. "First they tried to break down the individual," said one historian, "and then remold him as someone equipped to take over the world."

When Prescott graduated in 1917, he left Yale as something of a favorite son. He had been voted the most versatile member of his class and third in the category of most admired. Along with his prowess at baseball and golf, he won honors for his musical activities. He was ready to take on the world.

Then on April 6, 1917, with German U-boats stalking passenger ships in the Atlantic, the United States entered World War I—the war that would "make the world safe for Democracy," in President Woodrow Wilson's words. The senior class had listened intently to Wilson's speech declaring war on Germany, which ended with these words:

> [W]e shall fight for the things that we have always carried nearest our hearts—for democracy, for the rights and liberties of small nations . . . with the pride of those who know that the day has come when America is privileged to spend her blood and her might for the principles that gave her birth. God helping her, she can do no other.

When Wilson concluded the Congress rose as one and applause echoed through the chamber. Later, Prescott read that upon Wilson's return to the White House, he was heard to say, "My message was one of death for young men. How odd it seems to applaud that." And he put his head in his hands and wept.

At Yale, as on campuses across the land, career plans were put on hold. Prescott's Yale diploma was still in a roll, tied with a skinny red ribbon, when he enlisted in the field artillery. He couldn't wait to be a part of the grand adventure unfolding in Europe. This was a time when it was still possible to think of wars as righteous or even noble. When the national anthem was sung before a baseball game, and when it got to the part about the rockets' red glare and the bombs bursting in air, a person felt warm all over. And, at twenty-two, Prescott Bush did not feel young or innocent. What he felt was willing and eager to serve.

He was commissioned a captain in the field artillery, and in June 1918 his regiment landed in France. They were quickly thrown into the Meuse-Argonne offensive, in the neighborhood of Montfaucan, on the outer edge of Verdun. They were at the front for ten weeks, pinned down in the trenches for days. Only a sudden change in wind direction saved the captain and his troops from being gassed. If Prescott felt any fear, his letters home did not reflect it. "The noise is bothersome," he wrote, "and I will not offend your sensibilities by describing the lack of sanitary facilities. We are close enough to the enemy to see the sunlight glint off the barrels of their rifles."

The American Expeditionary Force, under General Pershing, soon had the Germans on the run. The Turks surrendered on the last day of October, after British troops under Field Marshal Allenby drove them out of Jericho, in Palestine, and Arab troops led by the adventurer T. E. Lawrence (Lawrence of Arabia) overran the port of Aqaba. Austria-Hungary surrendered four days later. The armistice was signed on November 11, 1918, and with the collapse of the German army, Kaiser Wilhelm fled to Holland.

Captain Prescott Bush served most of 1919 with the occupation troops in Germany, and years later, in his oral history, he would say of his service, "It was quite exciting and, of course, a wonderful experience." It was the type of experience his son would later endure in World War II when shot down in the Pacific and, to a lesser extent, his grandson would go through during the charged time of the sixties. (Although, the Vietnam War was by no means considered a "righteous" war as were World War I and World War II.) Also, the events of the time—the assassinations of Martin Luther King Jr. and Bobby Kennedy, the Democratic Convention riots, and the instability on campuses across the United States—contributed to an air of uncertainty.

Years later when George W. began to think about his options during his senior year at Yale, he joined the National Guard in Texas and trained as a fighter pilot. He received his commission in the summer of 1969. The principal speaker at the graduation ceremony was the congressman from Houston, George Herbert Walker Bush. He was the one to pin the silver wings on his son's chest. It was a very nice moment, one of which his grandfather would have been proud.

As a young businessman, Prescott Bush (at right) dressed for success.

Returning home after two years, Prescott doubted that he could buckle down to serious study again. Instead of going on to law school, as he had earlier planned, he started looking for a job, which he found while at Yale's first postwar reunion. On the advice of a classmate, he accepted a job with the Simmons Hardware Company and moved to St. Louis to become a management trainee. This was no one's idea of a dream job, but there were compensations. For a young man with the right credentials, it was possible to meet a charming class of people.

In fact, in the autumn of 1919, Prescott Bush met Dorothy "Dotty" Walker, a debutante with a face that might have been carved on a cameo, and the energy and inner strength of a champion athlete.

She was a graduate of private, all-girl schools in St. Louis and at Miss Porter's in Connecticut, as far as her education would go. Her father believed that sending a daughter to college was unladylike. Her schooling was designed to prepare her for being a debutante, training that was rarely so disdained by the beneficiary.

Dotty had natural political instincts, understood the privileged class, and in many ways was the conscience of her family. She would become, after all, the wife of a senator, the mother of one president, and the grandmother of another.

4

They Remember Mama

$\mathcal{D}$orothy came from tough, sturdy, high-achieving stock. Her grandfather David Davis Walker had built what may have been the largest dry-goods warehouse in the country, supplying corner and small-town stores throughout the Midwest and West. About 1890, D. D. Walker and his family began spending their summers in Kennebunkport, Maine, which has remained a regular family destination (for Walkers and Bushes) for vacations, pilgrimages, and political strategy sessions. Granddaughter Dorothy was born there in 1901, the second child (of six) of David's son George Herbert "Bert" Walker.

Bert Walker worked in the family business before starting the G. H. Walker Investment Company. He was a grizzly

The future Dorothy Walker Bush (age 3) in a rare restful moment.

41

bear of a man, a former Missouri heavyweight boxing champion, who intimidated his family as well as his business rivals. He enjoyed tussling with his own sons, who regarded him more with awe than affection.

"He was a tough father, a tough old bastard," one of his grandchildren, Elsie Walker, told Michael Kranish, a *Boston Globe* reporter. "There really wasn't a lot of love on the part of the boys for their father."

Much of his raw drive was a rebel-

George H. Walker serving in a posse June 1900.

lion against the life planned for him by his parents, Scottish Catholics who sent him to prepare for the priesthood. The schooling was stern, spare, and unforgiving, and it had the effect of driving the young man away from his religion. When he married a Protestant, his family refused to attend the wedding.

A fiercely private man, G. H. Walker would serve as president of the U. S. Golf Association, as Prescott Bush would after him. When a friend named Dwight Davis established the Davis Cup for tennis, Bert Walker donated a trophy to be awarded to the winner of an annual competition between British and American amateurs. The Walker Cup would become one of golf's prestigious tournaments.

For a man considered by some to be coarse, Walker had a side that embraced an almost royal life of grace and leisure. He enjoyed, in no particular order, drinking, gambling, golf, horses, a yacht, and speedboats. He sometimes traveled by private train. He maintained the estate on Walker's Point in Kennebunkport, Maine; a mansion on Long Island; an opulent apartment at One Sutton Place in Manhattan; and a ten-thousand-acre preserve called Duncannon in South Carolina. His properties were tended by an array of servants worthy of the Vanderbilts or Astors.

He adored Dorothy, so attractive and so organized and perhaps the best athlete in the family. Of course, that didn't help when Dorothy decided that she very much wanted to attend Vassar. Her father didn't believe in women going to college, thinking that it made them "argumentative." Despite her true wishes (and her own strength of will), she settled for Miss Porter's Finishing School in Connecticut, followed by six months in France with a friend.

It was after she returned from this trip that she met and was courted by Prescott Bush. Her father was impressed and receptive when Dorothy brought home this former Yale golfer and baseball star, a gangly young man of charm and elegance.

Prescott and Dotty were married in Kennebunkport, in the Church of Saint Ann's-by-the-sea, on August 6, 1921. According to an account in the society page, the altar was adorned with Japanese lilies

A view of Kennebunkport from the shore in Maine from 100 years ago.

and surrounded by pink gladiolas and larkspur. "The bride was charming," the report said, "in a gown of net embroidered with pearls and crystal over white satin." During the ceremony, the organist, a Mr. Waldo, played "O, Perfect Love." For a wedding present her father built them a bungalow within the family compound on Walker's Point. Dorothy would spend every summer there for the rest of her life.

Prescott and Dorothy were regulars on the court, although it was Dotty who was considered the most versatile athlete of the family.

She was a petite, dainty-looking woman, especially standing next to her strapping six-foot-four husband. References to her, then as now, tended to be soaked in sentiment, but the facts are strong enough. She won a tennis match while playing with a broken wrist. While campaigning for her son, she fell off her bicycle—at the age of almost eighty—and dislocated her shoulder. But the news was good, she told George. The doctor said she could probably ride her bike again in six weeks.

While Dotty and Prescott worked together in giving their sons and daughter a moral compass, she stoked their competitive fires. George recalls his mother asking about a tennis match he had played that day, and he replied innocently, "I thought I was off my game."

She jumped all over him. "You are just learning. You don't *have* a game. Maybe if you practiced more you'd have one."

In a wonderful example of Bush-ese, the future president said of the lesson learned, "Arrogance factor. Down. Determination to get a game. Up!"

George felt an overwhelming gratitude to his mother, who taught him about the joy and fullness of life. And from her he learned to be organized, to take risks, not to complain, to always strive to be better.

Years later Dorothy did what she had not done and had no need to do for four decades or more. Over the telephone, she scolded her second son, then the vice president of the United States, for what she perceived to be his rudeness during one of Ronald Reagan's State of the Union speeches.

Watching on television, as her son sat almost directly behind the president, it appeared to her that he was reading a book, or possibly even dozing.

"No, Mum," he protested. "I had my head down because I was following a printed copy of his speech."

George Bush accepts the vice-presidential nomination in 1988.

45

President George Bush in one of the last photos with his mother, the matriarch.

"I don't care," she said, rejecting his explanation. "It looked dis-respectful. I expect better of you."

"I'm sorry, Mum," he capitulated. "It won't happen again. From now on, I'll keep my head up."

She was carrying on for her husband, who had died in 1972, because in matters of political decorum Prescott Bush had the last word. His father was the commanding general, George always said, but make no mistake about it, his mother, his "Mum," was "the guy out there day in and day out shaping up the troops."

It is a distinctive trait among the Bush tribe, this business of referring to even their own mother as a "guy." But in truth Dorothy Walker Bush was one of the most thorough tomboys of her era. And athlete she was. She had placed second in a national girls' tennis championship in 1918, and she liked nothing better than to challenge a friend or relative to a one-mile swim in the frigid Atlantic Ocean. After the other swimmer quit, she would swim another mile. This was quite in keeping with the woman who was not only a fine athlete, but very much her own person, fully up to being the wife of a successful politician, manager of a busy household on which she stamped her own values, and raising a son who would be president of the United States—and father to another.

In May 1985 George wrote an essay for distribution within the family, meant as a gift for Mother's Day. In it he said:

She had five of us to raise—Pres, myself, Nancy, John, and Bucky—and she just felt strongly that there was too much for us to learn and to do to waste any time on chaos. So we had very little chaos around our house.

Physically, she is a small woman but made of mighty stuff. Nine months into her first pregnancy, she played in a (softball) game. Her last time up, she hit a home run and, without missing a base (I'm told), continued right off the field to the hospital to deliver Pres.

Then, twenty-five or thirty years later, near Washington, where my parents were then living, she was engaged in a hot team match in tennis. She fell on her wrist and was urged by her partner to default. No, sir. The match went on for some time in spite of the pain. Later they discovered she had broken her wrist.

She loved games and thought competition taught courage, fair play, and—I think most importantly—teamwork. She taught games to us endlessly. We learned from her everything we knew—solitaire, bridge, anagrams, Scrabble, charades, golf, swimming, tennis—you name it.

The sun (might have been) blistering hot, and she might have just come off the tennis court, have played a three-set match. But she would see one of us along the side, pining to play, and without even asking, there she would be, saying, "C'mon, let's go hit a few."

You would think she might have said, "I'm worn out; let me catch my breath." Not Mother. She would have us out on the court, hitting a few, just when we most wanted to learn to play. I can hear her now: "You can do it. You'll get the hang of it. You'll get it." And she would be patient and tireless, always absolutely sure we would— eventually—get it.

Among her principles she placed total honesty near the top, and she always expected the Bush offspring to have a concern for others. There was never any question about the absolute importance of those values.

"Although we knew Mother as a disciplinarian," continued George, "all of us knew she loved us profoundly. Part of that assurance came from what we called 'the giggles.' When we were with her, it seemed we always ended up unable to stop laughing.

"One morning at church, the Reverend Alfred Wilson was giving his sermon, and he took as his biblical text, 'Comfort me with apples.' For some reason, Pressie and I thought that was terribly funny, and we began to snicker out loud. Mother looked at us severely, and that quieted us—until suddenly the whole pew began to wiggle and shake, and there was Mother, attacked by 'the giggles.' Of course, looking at her broke us all up, and the whole Bush family had to beat a hasty and ignominious retreat, vanishing outside into gales of laughter.

"Dr. Wilson forgave Mother—I'm sure of that because Mum's whole life has been about faith. Her goodness, her kindness, her propensity to forgive, her love—all stem directly from her following the Bible and from her faith in God. Mother is a Christian. Her light really does shine.

"When Dad died of lung cancer—and, oh, how she loved him—she said to Nancy and to her daughters-in-law, 'Wear bright colors for the funeral. Your dad is in heaven. There is lots to be joyful about.'

"Probably the nicest compliment a mother can get is the affection and trust of a daughter-in-law. I know my wife, Barbara, has drawn strength, when times were hard, from Mother's indomitable sense of life as an adventure. Barbara calls her 'the most remarkable woman I have ever known.'"

Prescott was the statesman, Dorothy Bush the motivator and born diplomat. She made a point of according her daughters-in-law equal treatment, telling each of the four that she was her favorite.

"No, I was," says Barbara Bush, tongue firmly in cheek. "I really was. At least, that was what I thought based on how she acted toward me. She acted as if we were wonderful. All of us loved her. And she loved us."

It is interesting to note that independent and determined women have not been absent from the Bush family circles. Prescott married one, raised a daughter who qualified, and saw the wives of his sons excel in multiple ways.

Years later another inependent woman entered the scene when friends arranged a blind date for George W. with the dark-haired, bright-eyed Laura Welch, who grew up a few blocks from the Bush home in Midland. A private and calming soul, she won the

Dorothy and Prescott after his reelection
to the Senate in 1956.

nation's respect with her words and demeanor during the crisis after the attacks on the World Trade Center and the Pentagon.

They were married three months after that first date, a perfectly balanced couple, he the reformed playboy, she the former librarian. Imbued with West Texas common sense, she provides a calm and gentle restrait to her husband's sometimes impulsive ways.

When the forty-third president announced that he wanted the man behind the attacks, Osama Bin Laden, "dead or alive," her instincts may have suggested that the demand smacked of frontier justice. "Bushie," she said teasingly, "are you goin' to git 'im?"

It was Dorothy Walker, after all those years of standing by *her* man, who had passed on to her daughter-in-law Barbara the key to success for the wife of a politician. Barbara passed it on to her daugher-in-law Laura: "If you accompany him to a speech, and he asks for your opinion, no matter what, tell him he was wonderful."

One night, when George W. was running for governor of Texas, as he turned the car into the driveway, he asked Laura what she thought of his speech. Without hesitation, she replied, "It wasn't one of your best."

George W. turned toward her and stared and drove the car into the back end of the garage.

Even before his son settled in Texas, Prescott was saddling up.

Although independent women are more prevalent today, as the product of a more genteel era, trained to rise when a lady entered a room and to open the door if one wished to exit a car, Prescott Bush was sometimes befuddled by the strong women he encountered in politics.

It's not that he was entirely unused to strong women. After all, he had married one, and no one ever described George's wife, Barbara, as meek or unprepared to speak her mind. Once, not very long after marrying George, she was having a quiet smoke one night on the steps of the main house in Kennebunkport when Prescott joined her.

"That's not a nice habit for a woman," he said, lighting a cigar.

"I smoked before I became your daughter-in-law," she replied, "so you can't lecture me now."

In the 1952 Senate primary, he had to compete directly with Clare Boothe Luce, a noted playwright and the wife of Henry Luce, publisher of *Time* magazine and a former member of Congress. Mrs. Luce had the capacity to leave most men speechless. Prescott knew the feeling, when he learned that she planned to try to deny him the Republican nomination for the Senate. A delegation of state party leaders had promised it to him after the death of James O'Brien McMahon had created an unexpected vacancy. "If you will let us present your name," they had said, "you won't have to campaign for the nomination. We can guarantee that you will be the candidate on the first ballot."

This startling gesture was an acknowledgment of Prescott's ability to raise prodigious amounts of money for the party, as well as his efforts in two losing races, including one in the most recent Republican primary.

"I decided to do it," he said, "but no one was aware that Clare had ideas of barging into the picture. She was out in California someplace, and all of a sudden she reappeared, coming back to Connecticut and waging a terrific campaign to get the nomination. She thought she saw an opportunity to go to the United States Senate, but she was badly advised. She bought a lot of television and radio time, and the night before the convention, she rented the ballroom at the Bond Hotel, in Hartford, and held open house for all the delegates. They all went and ate her food and drank her beverages and had a gay old time.

"I didn't even have a headquarters. I stood out in the lobby of the same hotel and just shook hands with everybody as they came and went. The next day I received the nomination on the first ballot, as I had been assured I would. Clare Luce was very much disappointed by that event. After that, of course, I won the general election [against Abe Ribicoff] and went to the Senate.

"The next time she appeared, she had been nominated as our

ambassador to Italy. She dropped by the office to solicit my support for her appointment. She didn't have to do it, but I think that if she had not, some would have viewed this as an obvious slight.

"I don't usually worry about slights. Nevertheless, she came and was very cordial and, of course, I supported her on the floor when the nomination was presented. There was no opposition.

"After she had been over there a couple of years, she came back and I gave a luncheon for her in the Capitol. I had about twenty of the congressional leaders, of both houses—including Joe Martin, Charlie Halleck, Bill Knowland, Style Bridges, and Everett Dirksen. She was the only lady there. It was fascinating to me to see how she could hold the attention of all these political leaders and how deferential they were to her.

"So, after the luncheon she very graciously thanked me and we walked back to the Senate Office Building together. She said to me, 'Pres, you're a great senator. You have done a great job.'"

The compassion and energy of Dorothy Walker must have been a splendid asset for a quiet, stately man who found his great contentment in the Senate. In 1955 when Anne Morrow Lindbergh, the wife of Charles and a gifted writer, published a book called *Gifts from the Sea*, Dorothy Bush was one of the thousands of women who felt connected to the imagery and to Mrs. Lindbergh's quest for "grace . . . and inner harmony." She dropped the author a note:

Life gets so hectic that I just feel I am constantly in a jet plane, whirling through space. I am more determined than ever to let nothing interfere with our quiet little time for reading and prayer together each morning before Pres goes to the Senate.

Not even her children knew the extent to which she was involved in her husband's campaigns, at times by virtue of her spontaneity. In at least one instance, her quick reaction, despite her good intentions, invoked the law of unintended consequences.

In the summer of 1952, Prescott was smarting from the fact that his former partner, Averell Harriman, had placed the name of his opponent, Abe Ribicoff, in nomination at the state Democratic Convention. But he regarded Ribicoff as a principled man and looked forward to a campaign on the issues.

"Ribicoff was not given to dealing in personalities very much, any more than I was," said Prescott. "He was inclined to damn with faint praise. For instance, we both appeared at a big meeting before a largely black audience in Hartford, and I had a prepared speech. Abe came unprepared, as far as we could see.

"When he opened his remarks, he said, 'Of course, I listened with interest to Senator Bush. But I can't afford to have anybody write speeches for me.' Everybody laughed. He used that kind of dig, that kind of technique, and there was nothing mean-spirited there. I never worried much about him."

But the race was far from a lock. Ribicoff was getting a little mileage out of his campaign slogan, "You're Better Off with Ribicoff," and on the drive home to Greenwich, Prescott's campaign manager, Elmer Ryan, spotted one of his billboards.

"I wish we could develop something to offset that slogan," said Ryan. "That's pretty good: 'You're Better Off with Ribicoff.'"

From the backseat the voice of Dorothy Bush suddenly piped up: *"You're in a Jam with Abraham."* Elmer Ryan roared with laughter. He loved that line, and the next day the senator incorporated it into his speech. "Don't believe that sign that says, 'You're Better Off with Ribicoff.' The fact is, you'll be in a jam with Abraham." And the audience rewarded him with a nice, collective chuckle.

Unhappily, one thing followed another, as it often does in politics, and someone attached an ethnic connotation to the retort. Suddenly, that tower of tolerance, Prescott Bush, had to defend himself against the charge of being an anti-Semite.

"The editor of our local newspaper and his brother," he recalled, "both of whom were Jewish, came to see me at the house as soon as this appeared in print. They had received telephone calls from Hartford: 'What about Bush? Is he anti-Semitic?'

"So they dropped by to get the whole story. I told them exactly what had happened. They left perfectly satisfied. It was a one-day story, here today and gone tomorrow, because it should have been obvious that the remark was not meant to reflect some Jewish bias. I don't think I am that stupid, to do such a thing, even if I was so disposed, which I am not. My whole record speaks to that.

"I mean, if I had to defend myself, I would say, what about Abraham Lincoln? In much of his advertising he was Abraham Ribicoff. All I did was use his name for the sake of a rhyme.

"This type of thing does happen in a political campaign, and it is unfortunate. Abe Ribicoff, I am relieved to say, knew perfectly well that nothing cynical was intended or implied. We've been good friends for a long time. Whenever I go back to the Senate, he walks across the chamber to say hello."

An encounter with a less pleasant outcome took place in the 1956 reelection campaign. Thomas Dodd, then in the House, accused Dorothy Bush of lying after she criticized his record during a speech in Norwich, Connecticut. She had also mentioned that her husband had coauthored a flood prevention act, which she referred to as "the Bush-McCormick Act."

Prescott had said the bill had been of significant benefit to the state of Connecticut. Dodd said there was no such act and that the whole business was a fraud and Bush should be ashamed for trying to claim credit for an act that did not exist, and that Mrs. Bush knew better, too.

Now politicians can call each other corrupt, or even accuse another of burning down an orphanage, but you never, ever call the wife of a distinguished gentleman a liar. Prescott choked down the urge to pistol-whip Thomas Dodd and instead, with his staff, began to comb through the *Congressional Record*.

"Fortunately," he said, "we were able to produce copies of the *Record* where members of the Democratic Party had referred to this bill as the Bush-McCormick Act. John C. McCormick was then the leader of the Democrats in the House of Representatives, and he himself had called it the Bush-McCormick Act.

"We made all this quite clear in subsequent television ads during the campaign, and it put Mr. Dodd in quite a bad hole. He was willing to make reckless statements, and I formed the opinion—which I haven't changed—that he was an unreliable sort of person. Subsequent events rather confirmed that opinion, I think. [Dodd] was censured by the Senate in June 1967 for using campaign funds for his personal benefit.

"I didn't like Dotty being in the line of fire," Bush said, "but she rather enjoyed it. For the length of the campaign, we moved to Hartford because it was easier to travel around from there. Hartford was the political center of the state. The news agencies, the Associated Press and others, were all based there, and the Hartford newspapers had the largest circulation in Connecticut.

"We kept an apartment in a little hotel that we also had rented in 1952. The dust was still on the mantelpiece that had been there four years earlier, and we could identify some of our fingerprints.

"During the last few weeks of the race, Mrs. Bush had a car and a driver, and the campaign committee scheduled her to speak in different parts of the state. She was recognized at the end of the campaign as one of the most effective speakers the state had ever seen.

"She had taken lessons in elocution in Washington, in a class of twelve to fifteen women. She was graduated Number 1. So she was very helpful, and this really endeared her to the people around the state, especially the Republicans on whose behalf she most frequently spoke.

"She was able to memorize her speeches and gave them beautifully. She could stand up and talk for twenty minutes without looking at a note. She was very, very good."

Some thirty-two years later, Dorothy Walker Bush went back to Washington, D.C., to watch her son inaugurated as the forty-first president. The next day she paid a visit to him in the Oval Office, "the most wonderful day of my life. But I felt sad that his father wasn't there, too. How I wished he could have lived to see George become president."

When her son's distaste for broccoli became public—asked early in his term to list some of the privileges of the office, he had replied, "I don't have to eat my broccoli anymore"—she did not exactly bristle, but she did adjust the record. "He said I made him eat broccoli and he didn't like it. I don't remember any scenes about it. All he had to do was speak up."

In a lighthearted vein, the episode illustrates how incredibly easy it is to make news in the nation's capital. The president received complaints from the nation's broccoli growers but would not take back his comment.

On her historic weekend in Washington, Dorothy was the center of a protective shell formed by her five children and most of her sixteen grandchildren and twenty-two great-grandchildren.

George and Barbara named their youngest child after her: Dorothy "Doro" Bush, now Mrs. Bobby Koch.

"My first memories were of my grandmother, at Walker's Point," says Doro, "having iced tea with her and just sitting and chatting. I was just old enough to climb rocks, which the kids did forever. She kept an eye on us, but she never worried. We would go out in the boat with Dad, no matter what the weather was, even if it was stormy, and we'd have wild rides out there. She never batted an eye."

As a student at the country day school in Maine and at the Mary Institute, Dorothy Walker was always good at math. This proved helpful when she counted her blessings.

"Pres and I were fortunate to have five healthy children," she said, "all of whom had happy marriages and lives. Our family has been close and congenial. I loved being in Washington when Pres was in the Senate, but I loved our home in Connecticut, too. We were lucky to have done so much in our life together. But I suppose the highlights are the children.

"I learned from my mother that prayer was an important part of

Senator and Mrs. Prescott Bush (center) surrounded by their children and grandchildren.

one's daily life. I think that helped me greatly. Pres was a strong and wonderful husband who had a dry sense of humor. I was very lucky. Whatever challenges we had always proved to be small problems in the end."

Dorothy had a sister two years older than she, Nancy, who never married. Then came G. H. Walker Jr. ("Herbie"); Jimmy, who died in 1998 at age ninety-one; Louis; and John, a noted surgeon in internal medicine.

John's son, John M. Walker Jr., is a federal judge in New York City. He recalls the love and sense of security his aunt Dotty generated. "She led by the force of her personality," he said. "I'll never forget the day I was late getting to the airport, about an hour away. She guided me through those back roads of Maine to get me to the flight on time." Grizzly Adams could hardly have done it better.

Said her son George, "She lived the values she taught us. She did not want us to talk about ourselves, whether it was in sports or in life generally. She set examples when we were young by being a great competitor but always a great sport. She was always the one who picked up the guy who was hurt."

Newly elected President Bush and mother (seated) greet family and friends the day after his inauguration.

Lovingly, Prescott Jr. paid her this tribute on her ninetieth birth-day in July 1991: "She is one in a billion. She was always there when we needed her but never kept us tied to her. Mother was, and still is, a beautiful woman who was a role model for her sons in looking for the women we would marry.

"She is still the center of our family, radiating love to all, interested in what each of us is doing, thrilled with each grandchild and each great-grandchild."

"Mum never gave advice," says Prescott Jr.'s wife, Beth, "though I'm sure she must have bitten her tongue a million times to keep from doing it. She never criticized the wives of her sons. Can you imagine that?"

At the Bush compound in Kennebunkport George sits with the ladies. Barbara is all the way to the left and Dorothy is seated in front.

Beth recalled an almost spellbound moment, given her age and family position, when it was Dorothy's turn to read the Psalms aloud at her Bible study group. She had been absent for some weeks because of illness, and there was concern about whether she would be able to manage. Her eyes were failing, and she could not read the words, but the memory Prescott had praised decades earlier served her once more.

In the hush that settled over the room, Dorothy Walker Bush began to recite the Twenty-third Psalm, her voice clear and rhythmic, almost musical.

"She knew it by heart, of course," said Beth. "Those who heard her say, gently, 'The Lord is my Shepherd,' knew then that he truly was." Dorothy died on November 19, 1992, at the age of ninety-one, in the family home in Greenwich, two weeks after her son had lost his bid for a second presidential term.

5

The Businessman

Even as he courted and married Dorothy in 1921, Prescott was hard at work on his new job with Simmons Hardware. Working from his base in St. Louis, Prescott roamed the country for the company. One of his tasks was to sell a factory that had been built to make saddlery during the war. Saddlery, he noted, was going out as fast as automobiles were coming in. He traveled out to the Tennessee plant, and in less than three months, he had it sold.

Around the same time, Simmons Hardware was acquired by the Winchester Repeating Arms Company, based in New Haven, Connecticut. The new management asked Prescott to stay on, but Prescott was less than enthusiastic. Events were taking place, both romantic and tragic, that would rearrange his universe.

His father, Samuel Prescott Bush, had taken over the Buckeye Steel Castings Company, makers of railway cars and other equipment. Samuel knew how to run a railroad and quietly built the family's wealth, moving them into a mansion in Columbus. He was also a power in the Democratic Party in Ohio, helping to pass a work-men's compensation law that endeared him to the state's labor unions. Life was good for Samuel and his family.

Then on September 4, 1920, tragedy struck. While Samuel and his wife, Flora Sheldon Bush, were out for a walk while on holiday at Narragansett Bay, in Rhode Island, she lost her footing and slipped in front of a car. She died instantly. Theirs had been a union that could not end except in death, and Samuel was devastated.

Samuel and Flora's marriage had set a glowing example for the next generation. Though his tireless work ethic often kept him on the job while she vacationed with the children, their letters—especially hers to him—rang with passion and affection. They did not appear to have a wide circle of friends, but as Flora once explained, "You and I are so much to each other, we do not need the others." In one of her last letters, a poignant one, she wrote, "I want you, need you more every year, and we must take good care of each other."

As time went on, nothing in the Bush family tradition has been more consistent or remarkable than the history of loving and stable marriages. Of Prescott's four sons, all were still living in 2002, and all were still married to the wives of their youth. Daughter Nancy's hus-band, Alexander (Sandy) Ellis, died in 1991.

Prescott shared his father's anguish. He also carried the added burden of guilt, torn between comforting his father and continu-ing to meet his own obligations. His engagement to Dorothy had been announced that summer, less than two months before his mother's death.

Once he and Dorothy were married, and with his father back in Columbus, alone and depressed, Prescott put aside his own ambitions to join his father and help run a small rubber company in which his father had a substantial investment. Within a year, however, the business had failed. This only added to the family's despair. The creditors hired Prescott to sell the company for whatever he could get.

It was while auditing the books that he discovered, to his pain, that the former owner had been skimming the profits. Prescott acted instantly to expose the larceny, earning a reputation for probity that would last a lifetime. At the time, though, he also received threats that led him to begin keeping a loaded revolver in his desk against the day the man came looking for him. He never did. The danger passed when the swindler was convicted and sent to prison.

Prescott sold off the company's assets to Stedman Products, which made rubber flooring for hospitals, banks, and other public buildings. Then he went to work for the new owners, and he and Dorothy moved to Milton, Massachusetts. He commuted for two years to the company's factory in South Braintree, located on what was then known as "Rubber Row."

Dorothy gave birth to their first child, Prescott Jr., in 1922. The story of that birth has become a staple of the family legend, telling how she played in a baseball game while having contractions and the next morning gave birth to her first son, a bouncing ten-pounder. A second son was born in 1924, in the couple's Victorian home on Adams Street, in Milton. (The street was named after John Quincy Adams.) The baby was named after his maternal grandfather, George Herbert Walker, known as "Pop." Walker's sons quickly tagged the infant as "Little Pop," or "Poppy."

Around the time of his grandson's birth, Dorothy's father left behind his own investment house in St. Louis and moved to New York

President Bush and his mother on a casual day in 1989.

in response to a job offer from a friend, railroad baron E. H. Harriman. This was the same Harriman who was immortalized in the movie *Butch Cassidy and the Sundance Kid*. In the film, each time the outlaws tried to rob the safe on the mail car, the stubborn postal clerk refused to open it for fear of offending the powerful E. H. Harriman.

Harriman's son, Averell, had no zeal for the railroad business, so E. H. backed him in the investment field and then looked around for someone to run it. The best candidate turned out to be a financial genius who had the ability to be ruthless: G. H. Walker. Averell would eventually become the ambassador to the Soviet Union and the governor of New York, but as the 1930s loomed, he was just happy to roam the world, setting up deals and leaving Walker in charge of the company soon to be known as Brown Brothers Harriman.

Walker needed executive help in his new position, and he turned to his son-in-law. In a convenient move, Prescott Bush had taken a job with U. S. Rubber, whose headquarters were in New York. He had settled his family in Greenwich, Connecticut, a scenic, upscale, and historic community an hour and fifteen minutes from Manhattan, on the New Haven Railroad. Prescott avoided the card games in the club car, read his newspapers, and studied his reports both ways.

The players were already in place at the growing firm on Wall Street. Prescott went to work behind a rolltop desk in the wood-paneled Partners Room, where the partners would gather after hours for a drink. Most of the men in this clubby atmosphere were Yale alumni, including Roland Harriman, his old chum from the Class of '17, and a fellow Skull and Bonesman. He was Averell's younger brother.

Prescott was groomed to run the investment half of what had quickly become the nation's largest private bank. Movie-star handsome, tall, and athletic, he was a rainmaker, earning his money primarily by charming and snaring potential clients. Influenced by his Republican blue-blooded in-laws, and his clients, who were—no surprise—rich and conservative, Prescott broke his democratic ties and declared himself a Republican.

Dorothy and Prescott with Prescott Jr., Nancy, and George on the steps of their first home in Greenwich, Connecticut.

Meanwhile his father-in-law, George Walker, was increasingly at odds with Harriman and other partners of the firm. One partner, Knight Wooley, wrote that Walker had "dangerous dealings" that could damage the company's reputation. The resulting split was no trauma for the man from Missouri, who never was keen on having partners anyway. In fact, he may have had the last laugh. As the 1920s went out with a roar—and a crash—he cashed out some of his stocks and sold others "short," thus profiting on the power dive the market took. When the Great Depression gripped the country with all its fury, Walker was one of the rare investors who became richer. (Another was Joseph P. Kennedy, who also sold early and sold short.)

As Walker left the company, Prescott Bush and his associates were fighting to keep it—and their own portfolios—afloat.

"Things began to crumble," he lamented, looking back. "The first big crash was in September and October 1929. We rocked along, and in 1930 there was quite a comeback, given the situation, and a building boom. Bethlehem Steel had their biggest year in history, as did a lot of other companies in construction.

"Then our firm (W. H. Harriman and Sons) merged with Brown Brothers in 1931, and the economy just crumbled. It was dreadful timing for a new enterprise. The Harrimans had to put up additional capital to keep the firm solvent and strong enough to go out and solicit business.

"To their everlasting credit, they never batted an eye about it. It turned out to be the best thing they could have done because the company turned out to be a gold mine for them."

The act was a generous one, and the survival of the company lifted everybody's boat. The bailout also left Prescott ready to prosper during the boom years after World War II, which in turn set him up for his later campaigns for the U.S. Senate. He always remained grateful to Averell Harriman, even after the two no longer spoke to each other because of political ill will.

Prescott's greatest financial success may have come when he helped William Paley buy a half interest in the Columbia Broadcasting System. The stock market had been dropping like a marble down a drainpipe all through 1931. Now, in January 1932, the Dow-Jones average was at eighty-nine! Many companies were in desperate trouble, if not already out of business, and CBS was in receivership.

Averell, who happened to be in the office that day, had stopped by Prescott's desk. "Bill Paley and Herbert Bayard Swope are on their way up. Come with me, and let's hear what they have to say."

Prescott, recalling the meeting, said, "Bill Paley had agreed to a price of five million dollars for his half interest, but he and his

Prescott Bush prepares to conduct committee business.

friends and associates could only come up with two and a half million dollars. They wanted to know if we would put up the balance.

"Averell asked me to check it out and said we would get back to them. By June, the stock market had sunk to forty-eight, and you really had to have a belief in this thing and its future to go out with a straight face and tell someone, 'Buy this stock.'

"Now, where did I acquire this faith? Two of my best friends at that time, and throughout my life, were Richard R. "Red" Dupree, who became the president and chairman of Procter and Gamble, and Stanley Resor, the head of J. Walter Thompson, the biggest advertising agency in the country. In the course of my travels, I had negotiated the sale of a soap company to Procter and Gamble for twelve million dollars. We got a nice commission on that, the firm did.

"Dupree invited me out to his house in Cincinnati, and even after the deal closed, we kept up our friendship. He would invite me out for a round of golf, and later we would sit around his swimming pool or in his living room and talk. I urged him to talk because he was ten years my senior and one of the most interesting business minds I ever knew.

"During one conversation, he said, 'Pres, if you ever get a chance to get into radio, on the right basis, jump on it. That's the coming medium. Tremendous impact.'"

When the deal walked into his office, Bush picked up a telephone and called his two friends, Red Dupree and Stanley Resor—one big in soap, the other in advertising. "Both said, 'This is what you have been waiting for,' and I went to Averell and reported that to him. I said, 'Look, we have to do this deal.' And he said, 'Fine. Go do it.'" Which he did.

Prescott was pleased with himself, as he had every right to be. Radio, he pointed out, was still in its infancy. The Radio Corporation of America had been formed as recently as 1920, the same year the first commercial station opened in Pittsburgh. The first boxing match was broadcast in April 1921, and the British Broadcasting Company went on the air in November 1922. A performance of the Metropolitan Opera was transmitted to 6 million listeners in January 1925.

What truly intrigued him was a casual remark by Bill Paley at a later meeting. Paley said scientists were perfecting an invention that would enable people to sit at homes and offices and view moving objects many miles away on their radios. For now they were calling this innovation *cinema-radio*.

"Wouldn't that tend to keep fans from attending football games," asked Prescott, "or boxing matches?"

"That might be the case," replied Paley, "but I know one sport that would not be hurt. Your game, golf, the one sport that cannot be enjoyed vicariously."

After Paley left the onetime Yale baseball captain wondered briefly what the impact might be on the transportation industry when it became unnecessary for anybody to go anywhere to see anything. But he was not troubled by the thought for long because he knew that the development was far, far in the future—if it became a reality at all.

Prescott Bush later served on the board of CBS, saw the company grow into a giant, and attracted new business to Brown Harriman (among them Dresser Industries, Prudential Insurance, and Trans World Airlines. He sat on their boards, and invested in their stocks).

He came to understand the power of television, as did few politicians of his era. Almost coincidentally he eased into the financial security it would take to enter into politics, even as the world was being set up for another major conflict in which his son George would eventually play a role.

∼≋∽

In everyone's life there is a summer of '42; Prescott Bush spent his on Wall Street, where nostalgia and romance are not the hot commodities they were in the motion picture that made the phrase symbolic.

A headline that landed on the front page of the New York *Herald-Tribune* in July of that year read: "Hitler's Angel Has 3 Million in U.S. Bank." The reference was to the Union Banking Corporation. Prescott may have been upset or alarmed by the disclosure—he was one of its seven directors. A person of less established ethics would have been panicked.

The story claimed that the bank held $3 million in deposits for a German businessman, described as a "financier" for Adolf Hitler. There was speculation that the account may have been intended for the later use of "Nazi bigwigs."

Buried in the databases that dealt with the Bush family political tradition, the article was rediscovered and reported in the Boston *Globe*, in April 2001, by Michael Kranish. He concluded in the article that the connection had represented a potential "embarrassment" for Prescott. No one actually knew what purpose the fortune had been meant to serve, or who controlled it. Possibly, the money had been socked away as a hedge against Germany's defeat.

Bush and his partners at Brown Brothers Harriman informed the government regulators that the account, opened in the late 1930s, was "an unpaid courtesy for a client. The situation," wrote Kranish, "grew more serious when the government seized Union's assets under the Trading with the Enemy Act, the sort of action that could have ruined Bush's political dreams." The phrase was an ominous one.

The client was believed to be a friend of Charles Lindbergh, according to Roland Harriman. Prescott Bush acted quickly and openly on behalf of the firm, served well by a reputation that had never been compromised. He made available all records and all documents. Viewed six decades later in the era of serial corporate scandals and shattered careers, he received what can be viewed as the ultimate clean bill.

A decade later when he ran for the Senate, his involvement in the bank went untouched by the press or his political opponents.

Earlier that year he had accepted the chairmanship of the USO (United Service Organizations.) He traveled the country over the next two years raising millions for the National War Fund and, as the Boston *Globe* noted, "putting himself on the national stage for the first time . . . (and) boosting the morale of U.S. troops." Out of adversity good things came.

6

———∞∞∞———

Giving Something Back

$\mathcal{A}$t the start of World War II, financially well established, Prescott's pursuit of a political career began to find traction. Public service was an idea that he had clung to at some level since his arrival at Yale. As a young man in the mid-1920s, he had become moderator of the Greenwich town meetings and held that post for seventeen years. The New England town meeting is a tradition that dates back to colonial times, and it was a superb training ground. Prescott practiced his politics at the grass roots, door-to-door, dealing with sewers and streetlights and cracked sidewalks and beer licenses for small cafés.

By the 1940s Prescott could afford to set his sights on higher targets. He began to lay the groundwork with his prodigious fund-raising for the Republican Party on both state and national levels, and by heading the USO War Fund campaign, while his son George was deciding to postpone going to Yale to enlist.

In the spring of 1942, the secretary of war, Henry Stimson, a Republican in FDR's cabinet who had served Taft and Hoover as well, spoke at the Andover commencement. He urged the graduates to continue their education before entering the military. The country would need them soon enough.

George found his father in a hallway outside Cochran Chapel after the ceremony. In keeping with the paternal rules, Prescott did not greet his son with words of advice. Questions were acceptable. He asked if Stimson had said anything to change his mind.

"No, sir," said George, "I'm going in."

Yale could wait. Duty and country could not. He also felt an obligation to his brother Prescott Jr., who had tried to enlist and failed the physical. A sturdy specimen, Pressy had blown out a knee playing football, and had been born with an eye that sagged slightly.

George in the cockpit of his Avenger, the *Barbara III.*

George enlisted in the Navy Air Force on his eighteenth birthday. He went on to become the youngest navy pilot ever and a recognized war hero. His Avenger had been hit before he dropped its five-hundred-pound bombs on a radio station on the island of Chichi Jima, six hundred miles from Japan, before bailing out from his burning plane. He ordered his two crewmen to do the same,

but heard no response. One was reported to have bailed out, but his chute failed to open. His squadron commander, Don Melvin, made a couple of passes to signal where his raft was, and George Bush swam for his life.

He never referred to his close escape—his hours bobbing in a raft, sick from having swallowed sea water, before submarine USS *Finback* plucked him out of the sea. When an officer on the sub spotted him through his binocu-

An alert crewman snapped this shot of George Bush being rescued at sea by the USS *Finback* in September 1942.

lars, he was passing the time by firing his pistol at the seagulls circling overhead, which tells you all you need to know about the cool nonchalance of George Bush, by then a lieutenant, junior grade.

His sons would eventually be aware of their father's military career and his rescue. His mother had cataloged enough clippings—she was a great scrapbook keeper—to remind them that there was once a great war and that their father took part in it. George W. remembers opening one of his mother's scrapbooks once and finding a piece of rubber glued to one page. It was from the raft that saved his father's life.

George's homecoming was a fitting spin of the wheel for a young couple who met in circumstances right out of the fiction of a more innocent and romantic era. George had spotted Barbara the moment he walked into a formal dance at the Round Hill Country Club, when both were home from school during a Christmas break. She had reddish hair and a vibrant smile. Nor was the attraction one-sided. She would later say that she had difficulty "breathing" whenever he walked into a room.

She was dancing with a friend of his from Deerfield, and he waited until the music stopped to ask for an introduction. The dance floor was one of the few places where George Bush ever felt unsure of himself, and he was especially uneasy when the band struck up something fast. The couple sat on the sidelines and talked the night away. They met again at a party the next night, at the Apawamis Country Club, and she was his date for the prom at Andover. When he saw her again, he would be wearing navy whites.

George and Barbara had planned to be married the week before Christmas, but that date was no longer an option. Instead, the wedding took place on January 6, 1945, at the First Presbyterian Church in Rye, New York. Many years later, Barbara recalled the event with a line that was classic: "I married the first man I ever kissed. When I tell this to my children, they just about throw up."

❧

With his son safely home, Prescott began to position himself to run for office. In 1946, after Clare Boothe Luce announced she would not seek reelection to the House, Prescott considered running for Congress. Roland Harriman, speaking for all the partners, nixed that thought, however, assuring him, "We need you more than the House needs you." In other words, a gentleman simply doesn't drop weighty business to run for the lower body.

A media-savvy Prescott Bush beamed weekly telecasts back to Connecticut in the mid 1950s.

The Senate was another matter. When a seat was vacated in 1950, Prescott jumped in. He campaigned hard and worked to shed his banker image. He brought the Whiffenpoofs in from Yale to sing at his rallies, as well as borrowing the Brooklyn Sym-phoney orchestra from baseball's Dodgers.

The Sym-phoney was a collection of musicians only a little less sophisticated than Spike Jones and his City Slickers. "I wanted people to say," Prescott explained, "that Pres Bush may work on Wall Street, but he tries to make things a little more fun."

The Whiffenpoof Society had long since moved beyond Yale and into the cultural lore of America. The Whiffenpoofs give concerts, tour the country during holidays, and once were featured at a banquet where a faculty member delivered a speech entirely in Latin. Woodrow Wilson, then the president of Princeton, also spoke.

As a rookie politician Prescott was not too proud to accept whatever help he could get. He lost the 1950 general election by less than eleven hundred votes to William Benton, a cofounder with Chester Bowles of the famed advertising agency that bore their names. Prescott was hurt, unexpectedly, by the religious issue, and particularly

Grandkids adopt a worthy cause, selling orange and grape drinks to finance Prescott's first senate campaign.

by a statement by Drew Pearson. Early in the campaign Prescott had asked his manager, Elmer Ryan, an Irish Catholic, if being a Protestant would cost him votes. "Of course not," Ryan cheerfully told him. "We look on Protestants simply as Catholics who flunked Latin." Then, at the last minute, broadcaster Drew Pearson predicted that Benton would win and claimed that Prescott Bush was "the president of the Birth Control League." On the Sunday morning before the election, leaflets were left in every pew in every Catholic church in the state. This issue was a particularly sensitive one in Connecticut, which happened to be one of only two states in the country where it was against the law to sell condoms.

The phone almost rang off the wall at the Bush home, where Dorothy and Prescott kept telling callers, "No, it's not true." He was not president of the Birth Control League. (The Bushes *did* support and donate to Planned Parenthood.) But despite their denials, Prescott lost—by a margin that set the Bush family record for closeness until his grandson, George W., would win the electoral votes of Florida by less than six hundred votes in the most bizarre presidential race in memory.

Two years later Prescott tried again, this time losing his party's nomination to Bill Purtell, a Hartford Republican who lost the race for governor. Frustrated, and spent from fund-raisers and stump speeches, and complaining that he had been in more motel rooms than the Gideon Bible, Prescott swore off politics.

Then, in what seemed almost a case of divine intervention, the state's other senator, Democrat James O'Brien McMahon, suddenly died, and the Republican power brokers begged Prescott to try for a third time. He resisted, telling them, "I've had it. I'm not going around the state again with my hat in my hand." But they were persuasive; the nomination was his for the asking.

Accepting the challenge, he labeled himself as a "moderate progressive" and ran against a young Democratic congressman named Abraham Ribicoff. And, with Dwight Eisenhower and Richard Nixon at the top of the ticket, he won. He also started an evolving family trend in phrasemaking and self-identity. In the 1988 presidential campaign, his son George Bush advocated "a kinder, gentler nation." In 2000 Prescott's grandson George W. portrayed himself as a "compassionate conservative." None would be accused of deceptive advertising.

In truth, Prescott Bush was sometimes too liberal for his party's conservative leaders. He was to the left of the GOP on numerous issues, as when he supported civil rights legislation, larger immigration quotas, and higher taxes.

A typical story about him was headlined, "Bush Says Tax Burden May Have to Be Bigger." In the text, he was quoted as urging the Senate to "have the courage to raise the required revenues by approving whatever levels of taxation may be necessary" to pay the nation's bills for defense, science, and education.

When Prescott ran for reelection in 1956, he came to a stunning conclusion: The leaders of his own party seemed to be working against him, even hoping for his defeat.

"I was amazed that they would take so small a view as that of a man who was trying to do his damnedest for the Republican Party. It was almost inconceivable to me that they wouldn't go all out," he later remarked.

Prescott asked the chairman of the Republican Senatorial Campaign Committee to allay his concerns by publicly stating that he would win, but, confirming his worst fears, the chairman refused. Worse, stories were leaked to the press saying Prescott Bush was the Republican most likely to be defeated. "It hurt like mad," he said. Again, just as in the Harriman episode, loyalty appeared to mean nothing. In the end he won reelection, but the experience left a deep bruise on him and his family.

His son and grandson would take to heart the lessons of the patriarch. It wasn't merely a case of toeing the party line. If you wanted a role in making the rules, first you had to win. So Prescott's heirs did what was required to overcome the conservatives' basic distrust of Yale men with moderate roots. The first to run for president would make a vow that he would later retract with regret: "Read my lips. No new taxes." And the next George would push the biggest tax cut in the country's history. And they never loaned their names to—or, heaven forbid, raised money to promote the goals of—Planned Parenthood. They may not have been hard-core in the stands they took, but they knew, at the very least, how to keep the conservatives sullen but not mutinous.

There is also a lesson in persistence in all their political careers. Although the Bush men have all lost the first race they've run, they always got off the mat, and each put himself in position to win the second time around.

While Prescott was about to go gunning for the Senate, George "Poppy" Bush was home from the South Pacific, a war hero—although that is not a phrase he would ever use to describe himself. He and

Barbara were living in veterans' housing, in a shotgun house on East Seventh Street, on an unpaved road that was a notch or two above living in a tent. A partition divided the house into two apartments. Their unit had one bedroom, a small kitchen and its own bathroom, which they shared. On the other side, a mother and daughter team entertained male guests well into the night. The bathroom was sometimes unavailable for uncomfortably long periods.

Prescott and Dorothy Bush (middle) saw two of their sons marry in the same week: George and Barbara (left) and Prescott Jr. and Beth Kauffman (right).

The George Bushes were then, as now, an attractive and popular couple. Both never forgot the groundskeeper at Yale, a man named Morris Greenberg, who once slipped a note under the door of their apartment, offering batting tips to the young first baseman. George did raise his average from the low .200s, or less, to the .280s, so the advice must not have hurt him.

George W. attended his first Yale baseball game when he was minus three months old. Barbara was in the sixth month of her pregnancy, sitting in the first row of seats near the dugout, cheering for her handsome young husband, who played first base and captained the team his senior year. She kept score, using all the right symbols and abbreviations, her marks so precise that her finished scorecard looked like a form of early Aztec art.

As captain of the '48 team, Bush proudly accepts the original manuscript of Babe Ruth's autobiography for the Yale library.

Out of concern for her well being, the coach of the Bulldogs, Ethan Allen, insisted that she move to a seat behind home plate, where a screen protected fans from foul balls. Ethan Allen was a kindly gent, a former outfielder who had played thirteen seasons in the majors with five teams. He had retired with a lifetime average of exactly .300 and became a big name in expensive furniture. Don't ask.

Prescott had played first base for Yale thirty years earlier and hit with more power, but George was more graceful around the bag than his dad. And it was George who met Babe Ruth a few months before the death of the New York Yankees icon in 1948. In a ceremony at home plate, George accepted the original manuscript of Ruth's autobiography for the Yale library.

"He had cancer of the throat," he recalled years later, "and his

Barbara and George with their first born, George Walker Bush.

voice was just a croak. I didn't wonder then why he picked Yale to receive his papers. I only knew that this was Babe Ruth."

Yale reached the finals of the College World Series in 1947, losing to California, whose star pitcher was Jackie Jensen, later a slugging outfielder for the Red Sox. The next year they lost to USC, whose batboy, a kid named Sparky Anderson, would gain his fame as a manager by winning the World Series with teams in both leagues—the Reds and the Tigers.

Turning one, and then two years old, little George W. was a

particular favorite of Mr. Greenberg's, who would take him to the ball field and other cultural centers, such as the Peabody Museum. One day, when bringing the little boy back home, he asked the lovely Mrs. Bush if she remembered seeing the dinosaur they had at the Peabody. She did, indeed. He handed her a paper bag. Inside were bones from the dinosaur's tail. Barbara discreetly returned the missing bones to the museum.

By 1948 George Bush had earned his degree in economics with honors (Phi Beta Kappa), and it was time to look for a job. He also hoped to find a more suitable environment for an active, almost rowdy two-year-old.

The only problem was that although the twenty-four-year-old navy veteran was in a hurry to find his future, he had no idea what it might be. He was certain of only one thing: It would not be on Wall Street. "I wanted to do something on my own," he said. "I did not want to be in the shadow of this very powerful and respected man."

George did have a job offer from Neil Mallon, the chairman of Dresser Industries. He wanted George to come and learn the oil business from the bottom up.

Mallon and Prescott had been in Skull and Bones together, and Mallon had known Prescott's boys most of their lives.

"We were all very fond of him," said George "Our son Neil is named after him. He was a great salesman. He convinced me to move to Odessa. I had no idea where it was. Had to look it up on a road map."

When George broke the news to her, Barbara, who had known only the gentility of the eastern seaboard, hesitated for just a heartbeat. "I've *always* wanted to live in Odessa," she said, smiling bravely.

So George headed for west Texas, where he would start at the bottom and really learn the oil business. Barbara and the baby would join him in Odessa once he found a house to rent.

As they prepared to move, the battered old Plymouth George had bought after his discharge from the navy finally broke down—with Barbara and the baby inside. Prescott called and offered to help him get a new car.

"He did that," guessed George, "because he didn't like the picture of Barbara stranded along the highway with the little one. So together we bought a red 1947 Studebaker.

"He didn't spoil us by giving us a lot of stuff. We were never conscious of his wealth. We were always conscious of his achievement and respect."

Those were boom times in the oil patch, with veterans returning home and many heading to the oil and cactus belt to seek their fortunes. George was hired at three hundred dollars a month to work for Ideco, an oil field supply company owned by Dresser.

He drove straight through to west Texas, past the endless miles of prairie, the monotony of the landscape unbroken by tumbleweed and sagebrush. He sent for Barbara and young George W. a week after he arrived.

The Ideco store was a tin-roofed warehouse. George earned his first paychecks sweeping floors and painting oil rigs and pump jacks in the broiling sun of a Texas summer. In time the company transferred him to California, where one of his jobs was selling drilling bits, traveling from rig to rig along a cluster of small towns—Compton, Whittier, Ventura and Bakersfield. Their daughter, Robin, blond, blue-eyed, and angelic, was born in Compton, and Prescott was making his way in Congress.

In 1950 the company moved them back to Texas, this time to Midland, a more suburban, white-collar town than blue-collar Odessa, in the heart of the Permian Basin. George was learning the language of the oil fields, and catching the fever of the spirited men who gambled whatever they had on finding the earth's treasures deep beneath the west Texas soil.

In 1953, with investment capital raised largely by his Uncle Herbie—George Herbert Walker Jr.—George cofounded the Zapata

The Phi Beta Kappa from Yale learns about oil rigs from the ground up in Midland, Texas, 1949.

Oil Company with the Liedtke brothers, Hugh and Bill. Subsequently, in 1959, they split the company in two, and George moved the off-shore operations to Houston. In time, Hugh Liedtke would turn his holdings into a company called Pennzoil.

But the ambitious, goal-oriented Bush had accomplished what he set out to do. He had made a million dollars before he was forty, and his family had made a series of moves into larger, more comfortable homes. By the time they left Texas, he was well known and well liked, part of Midland's moneyed class—but not, in his words, "big-league rich" by Texas standards.

The friends and partnerships he formed in Midland would be there for George the rest of his life, and vice versa. The lessons Prescott had preached about loyalty might as well have been branded on his chest like a sailor's tattoo.

His father had experienced both sides, had seen personal loyalty trumped by political priorities. Still, there was surprising warmth in the voice of Prescott Bush when he spoke of his former business part-ner Averell Harriman, considering that they had not talked to each other in many years. He was grateful, and always would be, for the actions of Harriman in pumping his family's money into the struggling investment firm during the Great Depression. This uncommon ges-ture helped both the firm and the partners to avoid being swept away by a rising tide of debt.

"By the mid-1930s," Prescott said, "Averell would rarely set foot in the office. He was becoming more and more powerful in the

Democratic Party. But his connections were definitely a mixed bless-
ing for the firm.

"First, the old firm of Brown Brothers used to sell traveler's checks,
and it was the only bank that did. When Woodrow Wilson went to
the peace conference after World War I, he carried with him a
Brown Brothers letter of credit. We established those banking connections around the world.

"But when the firms merged, the new company was immediately
bolstered by the impact of the Harriman connections abroad. Of
course, the financial community was not enamored of the New Deal,
in the early days, and the fact that Averell was part of it became a bit
of a hurdle. A big corporate client would say, 'What the hell is your
partner doing down there with those socialists?' We would laugh it off
and say, 'He has done a lot in industry and he wants to do something
for his country. If the president wants him to be his ambassador to
Russia, why, fine, he's going to do it.'

"You have got to have ambition to get anywhere in this business,
and he was very ambitious. He served at the highest levels of the
administration. Later you saw the pictures of Yalta and the confer-
ences in Africa, and there he was, standing right there beside
Roosevelt and Churchill and Stalin, all those fellows. He was later
ambassador to Britain, and he had a distinguished record: secretary
of commerce, administrator of the Marshall Plan, governor of the
state of New York.

"I believe he was a major contributor to FDR's campaign in 1932.
There were not many business executives who supported the New
Deal in those days, so he moved ahead pretty fast. His brother
Roland was a staunch Republican, but he minded the store. Never

did anything in public life until Truman appointed him to be the head of the American Red Cross in 1946."

Averell Harriman and Prescott Bush remained each other's well-wishers until 1952, when their political differences poisoned their friendship. There may be room, even a need, for strange bedfellows, but a lifelong friend does not make a conspicuous display of public regard for his friend's adversary.

"Averell had made the nominating speech for Abe Ribicoff at the Democratic convention, and I was frankly quite disappointed. We had been partners for many years. There was no blowup. We just stopped speaking. I have always believed that the loyalty to a friend trumps any obligation to a political party. You do what your conscience tells you in private, but in public you remain neutral, at the very least.

"But Averell did me one favor. The support he gave Ribicoff kept Abe from making the obvious attack on the rich Wall Street banker. When I ran against Thomas Dodd in 1956, he said during one debate, 'I notice Senator Bush seems to have a lot of time to play golf. I can't afford to play golf.' By inference, he was saying that 'Bush is a wealthy fellow who hasn't got much to do, whereas I'm the poor struggling fellow who has to work all the time.'

"Then someone in the audience asked what *his* hobby was, and Dodd replied, 'horseback riding.' When it was my turn to speak, I said, 'Well, I congratulate my opponent. I have never been able to afford a horse.'"

What Prescott perceived as an even more hurtful act of disloyalty took the form of a secret attempt by leading Republicans to sabotage his campaign in '56, even at the expense of electing a Democrat. He was grouped in the Senate with Clifford Case of New

Jersey and Leverett Saltonstall of Massachusetts, as Republicans who were classified as liberals. They had lent a hand in fighting reactionary southern Democrats on civil rights legislation and supported federal aid to the poor and dispossessed, and other causes not entirely popular in the upper ranks of the party.

When Prescott confronted the Connecticut state chairman and asked him to issue a statement

Senator Prescott Bush's official photo.

predicting a Bush victory in the coming election and the chairman refused, Prescott knew beyond any doubt that he had been targeted by his own party. To a man who had stressed to his children that loyalty was one of life's essential virtues, this was a stunning blow. This may or may not have been a factor in his decision not to run again in 1962, but it surely took some of the joy out of serving for the next six years.

To the Bushes, loyalty was not a word to be inflated like a balloon; it was and is a way of life. This fierce sense of loyalty within the family was exhibited by George W. when working on his father's 1988 presidential campaign, when Lee Atwater, whose consulting firm represented rival Jack Kemp, was brought aboard. When Atwater had done his dance and asked if there were any questions, George W. said, "Yes, I have one. How are we supposed to trust you?"

Atwater sort of blinked and said, "Are you serious?"

George W. replied, "I'm damned serious, pal. In our family, if you go to war, we want you completely on our side. If George Bush is in the room and a hand grenade rolls across the floor, we expect you to fall on it. We love George Bush and, by God, you had better bust your ass for him."

Atwater issued his own challenge: "If you feel that way, why don't you come up here and keep an eye on me? And if I'm disloyal, you can do something about it."

That pleased George W., and he said he might do that. The invitation appealed to him on more than one level, but first he had to refine his exit strategy from a crashing oil business. He had serious thinking to do.

Being out of the oil business, George W. was excited about moving to Washington, D.C. He relished the prospect of working for his father as an adult and being involved in a national campaign, at the top of the ticket, with the stakes so high they were off the meter.

Then, in October 1987, along came *Newsweek*, with George Bush on the cover in a speedboat and a caption under the photo that read, "Fighting the Wimp Factor."

The son was incensed. This was George Bush, the youngest pilot to get his silver wings in the Navy Air Force in World War II. He safely crash-landed a plane carrying four 600-pound depth charges in its belly into the water. (That's no small feat.) Another time he was shot down and rescued by a submarine within swimming distance of a Japanese occupied island. In all he flew fifty-eight missions and won the navy's Distinguished Flying Cross by the age of twenty-one. How could they? A man who had served his country as director of the CIA, as a special envoy to China, and as the ambassador to the United Nations, not to mention head of the Republican National

Party during the Watergate crisis, when he had to fight like hell to keep the party from sinking into the primeval ooze. *That* George Bush! How could they?

The cover story was written by Margaret Warner, a fine lady and gifted writer, someone George W. respected. She called after his bellows of outrage had frightened all the ducks off the Potomac.

He wasn't kind or diplomatic. "This is disgraceful," he snarled. "You spent all this time to write a two-page article, and it had the word *wimp* in it seven times about George Bush?" He was furious, but he lowered his voice to a chill.

As he recalled the conversation later, the writer blamed the caption on her editors and said she didn't write the cover copy, which was undoubtedly true.

George W. was unmoved. "Then you ought to quit," he said. "You ought to quit if that's the kind of journalistic integrity you have."

George W. gets a pass, a press pass, on that one. What the media saw as suspicion on his part was simply his way of rating them on the fairness scale. He was in charge of screening journalists. They would come in asking for interviews, some well meaning and some not. His opening gambit was, "Why you? Give me one reason why I should let you interview George Bush."

As for the rest of the job he was to do for his father, he had no title and no need for one because no candidate had created a job exactly like this one. He would take on whatever tasks needed doing, under any kind of conditions. He was the eyes and ears, the secure line to anywhere. He was the loyalty inspector, the B.S. detector, the guy with no agenda except to see his father win. He could even make speeches or appearances when his schedule had an overload—you want a George Bush, you get a George Bush! In a pinch, he could crack heads, but no one would know, not from him. He didn't need to pad his résumé.

The loyalty that George W. showed to his father during his first presidential campaign is the loyalty that all the Bushes exhibit. It is a trait that was passed down from Prescott, who demonstrated his loyalty many times, including in 1956 when President Eisenhower

The two Georges stroll the grounds at Camp David.

pleaded for him to oppose an amendment to the Social Security Act that the labor unions had strongly supported. The act would make a worker who was disabled on the job eligible for full benefits at the age of fifty, instead of sixty-five. Prescott had won the respect of the unions in Connecticut, and he was sympathetic to the bill.

Ike sent Marion B. Folsom, his secretary of health, education, and welfare, to convince Prescott that the bill was a budget-buster and the timing was wrong. Ike needed Bush and his credentials, he said, to attract the votes that were then on the bubble.

Prescott had two problems. He was running for reelection in Connecticut, where the amendment was popular, and his colleague, Bill Purtell, had come out in favor of it. However, Ike was the president and leader of the Republican Party. When the roll was taken, Bush would not defy Ike.

7

The Honest Broker

A favorite slogan in the 1952 presidential campaign was "I like Ike," and the fall election proved its merit. Dwight D. Eisenhower, acclaimed as a war hero, took the White House in a landslide, beating Adlai E. Stevenson with a record thirty-three million votes.

On his coattails came enough new Republican members of Congress that their party would now control the government for the first time in twenty-four years. One Pennsylvania housewife remarked, "It was like America had come home." Everything was coming up roses for the Republicans.

It wasn't long, however, before the thorns in the rose bed became apparent. Enter Prescott Bush. One of the twelve new Republican senators, Prescott had the best training a new senator could have—short of being able to defuse a land mine. Forthright and ethical, Prescott was a deal-maker, a man who knew how to bring adversaries together, even if one of them was not a willing buyer. His skills would be needed.

Senator Robert A. Taft of Ohio, son of William Howard Taft, twenty-seventh president and tenth chief justice, had been in the Senate since 1938. By the 1950s he had gone beyond his distinguished pedigree to establish a solid record as a highly talented and always firmly conservative player in American politics. He also knew his own mind, was always his own man, and could put up a fearsome battle in defense of his positions—faithfulness to his cause being even more important than winning. He won respect from many, including those who didn't always agree with him. John F. Kennedy devoted a chapter to Taft in his Pulitzer prize–winning book, *Profiles in Courage*.

Nevertheless, Taft could be a real thorn in the side for a president, as Eisenhower's predecessors had learned. Taft opposed Roosevelt's New Deal and his interventionist foreign policy, before Pearl Harbor. Harry Truman had felt the sting of his opposition as Truman tried to deal with America's postwar economic problems, labor troubles, and the crisis in Korea.

Taft had coauthored the Taft-Hartley Act, to limit union activities, encouraged Wisconsin senator Joseph McCarthy's early Red-hunting activities, and condemned Truman's entry into Korea without a formal declaration of war as unconstitutional. Taft's positions infrequently prevailed, but he was always faithful to his conservative values. In his devotion to principle, Prescott Bush sided with the stern Ohioan, quoting Edmund Burke in his famous remark to the voters of Bristol: "Your representative owes you not his industry only, but his judgment; and he betrays instead of serving you if he sacrifices it to your opinion." And Taft could make life difficult for his opponents.

The *Times* of London summed him up this way:

He fully deserved his reputation for honesty and candor. With all of his remarkable gifts for assembling and sorting facts, he had an even more striking capacity for drawing conclusions that seemed to be based on tacit assumptions that American life was at its best about 1910.

Over the years Taft had become an increasingly dominant, if not exactly unifying, figure in his party. He was known as "Mr. Republican." Three times he had been a contender for its presidential nomination, and he had wanted to run again in 1952. But this time even many of his friends felt that Eisenhower should be their man.

Prescott Bush, who had known Taft on a friendly basis for many years and had supported some of his previous campaigns, was among them. He met with Taft and told him honestly that he thought the party had a better chance to win with Eisenhower. This could have soured their relationship, but fortunately, as Prescott described it later, "[Taft] made no objection, and it never came up again."

As Eisenhower settled into the White House, the standing gag that explained his popularity was, "The people like a president who doesn't meddle in the affairs of government." Taft had no problem with the idea of less is better. Outwardly, the two men seemed fairly quickly reconciled.

Eisenhower appreciated the senator's political acumen, his effective leadership, and his support of such controversial matters as the nomination of Charles E. Bohlen as ambassador to the Soviet Union—an appointment bitterly opposed by Senator Joe McCarthy and his allies.

But there continued to be deep-seated tensions and differences between them that might not be bridged. Ike was beloved by the American mainstream; Taft owned the hearts of conservatives. The Republican Party elders were desperate to see them stand united. But it would not be easy. Eisenhower turned out to be less conservative than liberals had feared, and Taft was more of an absolutist, one who would not surrender a point of principle, especially on a core issue like a balanced budget.

Part of the problem was, simply, Eisenhower's shaping by his long military career. Prescott analyzed it this way: "As commander-in-chief of operations in the European theater, he didn't have to consult too much with other agencies. In his military experience, he was always on top and everybody else was down here."

Prescott also saw Eisenhower as not wishing to get his hands dirty. "Ike was a bit timid at first about politics," Bush observed. "He sort of visualized, I think, that he didn't want to get down into the strongly partisan aspects."

Whatever the reason, Eisenhower was slow to appreciate that the nurturing of senators was a perfectly reasonable thing to do. As Prescott put it, "He didn't quite appreciate the fact that while the Constitution gives the president tremendous authority, it also provides for a government of checks and balances, and the Senate has the principal burden in that tripartite setup."

Though his leadership during World War II was the basis of Ike's fame and postwar popularity, now that he was back in the civilian world and into the new arena of Washington politics, his conditioning led to problems.

He was slow to reach out to Taft and his supporters. After all, in the army you didn't jump over the net to congratulate every opponent you defeated. Yet the greatest single blow of Taft's national political career was his narrow defeat by the general, after a bitterly fought contest at the Republican Convention in Chicago in July 1952. Now he faced the challenge of working *with* the general.

In this domestic political arena, the outstretched hand was needed. Eisenhower's failure to understand this got him off to an uneasy start with Taft, as well as other Republicans.

A case in point occurred shortly after the election. Taft, who was then Senate floor leader, and Eugene Milliken and Styles Bridges, important Republican committee chairmen, called on Eisenhower at his home in New York where he had been serving as president of Columbia University. When the senators left, it was with the impression that some pretty definite arrangements for cooperation had been agreed upon.

Then back in Washington just before the inauguration, a runner brought a message to Taft in the Republicans' private dining room in the Capitol. The note said that Martin Durkin was designated to be the secretary of labor. Prescott happened to be dining with Taft and his colleagues that day and later described the response:

"Taft nearly exploded at this news because he had not been consulted at all. He was the senior Republican on the Labor Committee, the author of the Taft-Hartley Act, the leader of the Senate whose support for nominations was the most necessary of all. He just said, 'This is incomprehensible! It is incredible that this appointment could have been made without consulting any of us.'"

Apparently not even the senators from Michigan, the new labor secretary's home state, were aware of the decision. This was just not the way things were done in Washington, and it made for a rough transition for the new president. This was especially so because the leader of the Senate had just pledged himself to support Eisenhower, and his policies, in the interest of the party and the country.

As Prescott described it, "The Republican senators grew restless. Some of them became quite sore at the Eisenhower administration because, after being out of power for so long, they didn't feel they were getting the recognition that should have been theirs. Some felt they were being ignored in connection with the appointments, and favors, the White House was in a position to grant. They were out-spoken about it around this lunch table day after day."

This was inside baseball at its best and worst, a glimpse inside the corridors of power and pettiness. Prescott Bush found himself com-muting regularly between Ike's ivory tower and Taft's lighthouse for the true believers.

If George W. Bush has it in his genes to be, in his words, "a uniter, not a divider," he inherited this trait from his grandfather, the unof-ficial referee in the tense months when the Republican Party's two most influential figures were sparring. Not in his father's term as pres-ident, nor in his own first year or two in the office, did there exist a situation close to what was then called, and not for the last time, "a battle for the soul of the party."

In the last fifty years there has not been a president as popular as Eisenhower who had to contend with a statesman of Taft's stature, the symbol of what was then, and still is, the GOP's dominant wing.

Keep in mind, too, that most of the power struggles of that era took place behind closed doors, and the country learned of them months or years later, if ever. This was the last era before television beamed its eye everywhere and "gotcha" journalism became common.

Prescott felt obligated to come to the aid of his party. This is what friends do. Sherman Adams, the White House chief of staff, was taking a good deal of abuse, as a chief of staff frequently does. This enabled the senators to avoid taking the distasteful and dangerous step of pounding Eisenhower himself.

They felt that Adams, who was an experienced politician, a former governor of New Hampshire and a former congressman, was in a position to guide Eisenhower better than he was doing. But they suspected that Adams was playing the game that the president wanted to play, keeping him remote from the core, practical phases of politics.

Adams was a tough-minded bantam of a man, about five feet eight. His official title was assistant to the president, but he described his duties as "management of the president's desk." Attempting to overcome the tensions and strengthen cooperation between the Oval Office and the Senate, Prescott cultivated the friendship of this man often judged to be brittle and difficult and before long had established a rapport with him.

Perhaps because he wasn't hampered by the resentments carried by some of the other senators, Prescott was able to make minor requests to which Adams was responsive, taking pains to avoid making any that might be viewed as unreasonable. And through working this way with Adams, Prescott was able to develop an agreeable relationship with the president.

That winter and spring Eisenhower began inviting Prescott to play golf with him. The president was a devout golfer. One of his early actions as president had been to have a putting green installed on the White House lawn. Heading for the links was a valued escape for him, but it also could be a valuable opportunity for anyone, legislator or businessman, who qualified to be invited to play along.

Happily, Prescott also loved the sport and played an excellent game, with a 2-handicap, as well as having proved himself thus far through his dealings with Sherman Adams. So through that most social of American pastimes, he became a quiet but logical choice to serve as a go-between or, in his own modest assessment, a messenger.

The connection worked because he strictly abided by a rule he set for himself: "I never talked to the press about what the president said on the golf course. Nor did I share his thoughts or comments with anyone else, unless I had reason to believe he wished me to do so."

Prescott thought he saw a chance to ease the tensions when he had a visit from William Taft, son of the senator and a professor at Yale and therefore a Connecticut resident and a constituent of Prescott's. The younger Taft was interested in being appointed as ambassador to Ireland.

Ireland has always been a popular post, and others were seeking the job, but Prescott saw the younger Taft as a strong choice. For one thing, he was an accomplished student of the Gaelic language, as well as being the son of a senator and grandson of a president. And this was certainly an opportunity for some political fence-mending. Prescott went to Senator Taft and asked how he would feel about his son being appointed ambassador to the Emerald Isle. Taft hesitated a moment, then said, "Well, they could look around for a long time without finding a better qualified man." Prescott took that to mean that he looked on the idea with favor, so he submitted the name of William Taft to the White House.

He was annoyed when he didn't hear back in a reasonable length of time. He had checked once or twice, asking if the matter was being considered, and was told that it was. Then after a month or so had passed, Senator Taft's administrative assistant dropped by Prescott's office on a Saturday morning and left a message with his executive secretary: "Senator Taft is mad as a hornet. He had been given to understand that this appointment of his son was to go through. This long delay indicates to him that there is some uncertainty about it, and he is really fit to be tied. He thinks it is almost a personal affront to him. I think your senator needs to know about it."

An agitated Prescott picked up the phone and called Sherman Adams. "Sherm," he told him, "you're in trouble with our majority leader on this Taft nomination to Ireland. This thing has gone too far. I suggest that you get that name down here before noon today, or else you are going to have to explain it to our Republican senators, who are strongly behind Bob Taft. And it's a darned good appointment anyway. Should be made."

Before noon Adams called back to say that the name was on the way down to the Senate for confirmation and that Senator Taft's office had been notified. (If such matters strike the outsider as petulant, the fact remains that this is how the system works, an insight into how smaller vouchers are cashed, clearing the way for the larger ones to follow.) A month later a dinner was given in honor of William Taft by the former ambassador to Ireland, George Garrett, and his wife, Ethel. In front of thirty-two guests, Senator Taft stood and thanked Prescott, without whom, he said, "this occasion would not have happened." While Prescott appreciated the praise, it was not what he intended. He had wanted Eisenhower to be in the position to do Bob Taft a courtesy, a kindness.

"When a proud man asks for a favor," said the honest broker, "and a proud man grants one, both have taken a step toward understanding. They have improved the chances of forming a bond."

There was one dramatic blowup still to come between the two rivals for the soul of the Republican Party, in mid-1953, but nevertheless, in time they came to achieve what Eisenhower referred to as a "curious friendship." During 1953 Taft also puzzled his friends by appearing testier than ever and at times more erratic. As it turned out, he was struggling with more than politics. He was also more seriously ill than he, and they, could realize. Prescott discovered this, to his terrible surprise, when he helped to organize a dinner at the Burning Tree Golf Club, sponsored by the new senators to honor the two majority leaders, Taft and Styles Bridges. Prescott happened to be the only member of the club among the freshmen, so he was appointed the dinner chairman.

In that capacity Prescott went to see Taft, to plan the dinner. "First I asked him if a certain date was convenient to him," Bush said later. "He replied, 'No, I have a speaking engagement in Rochester that night.' I said, 'What in the world are you doing, with all that you have to do, going up to Rochester to make a speech? There's no campaign going on, so what's this all about?'

"He said, 'The fact is, they are paying me five hundred dollars to make this speech, and I am very pressed financially. With Martha's illness'—she had suffered a stroke—'our resources are rather strained and, frankly, this money is helpful.'

"We found another date for the dinner, but I was saddened by that sidelight. Taft was supposed to come from a very wealthy family, with old money and all, and in truth he was struggling to pay his medical bills. Wasn't close to being a wealthy man. I don't think he left much of an estate."

Taft's wife was quite ill after her stroke. Prescott always remembered the occasion when he and his wife had dinner with the Tafts at their Georgetown home. "I remember he had to carry his wife in his arms to the dinner table. It was really quite moving. One side of her face was paralyzed, and her body was immobilized. It was very sad. Strangely enough, she outlived him by quite a long time, because he died in August of that year, 1953.

"I heard through a mutual friend of mine, who was close to the director of the hospital, that Bob Taft had an incurable cancer. No one else in the Senate knew about it. I couldn't carry this around, so I went to Senator Bricker, who was his close and good friend, and told John. He was shocked and upset.

"But Taft was in such terrible shape there wasn't time to do anything for him. The end came within weeks."

The cancer took Taft's life on the morning of July 31, 1953. Among the tributes was this one from President Eisenhower: "The Senate has lost one of its leading members of all time. The American people have lost a truly great citizen, and I have lost a wise counselor and a valued friend."

After Taft's death, a testimonial dinner was held at Burning Tree Golf Club, and the president attended. Prescott provided the entertainment by getting the Yale University close harmony group, the Whiffenpoofs, to sing. Prescott's son Jonathan was among them, a first bass.

As Prescott later recalled, "Eisenhower was very pleased with them, and he stuck around after dinner while the boys sang informally for him in the locker room. For a long time after that, whenever I would see the president, he would ask, 'How's Johnny?' It was amazing, this little incident. I had four sons, and he never knew but that one, but he always remembered Johnny and his crowd."

Despite his political awareness and bridge-building gifts, however, Prescott had his own learning to do as a freshman senator. And there were yet other strong Senate personalities with whom he would have to cope.

When arranging the dinner at Burning Tree Golf Club, Prescott unexpectedly ran into one slight wrinkle: Their rules at the time barred women from the premises. In the traditionally all-male world of Capitol politics, that might not even have been something to think about. But now there was a female senator, Margaret Chase Smith of Maine, and she wasn't someone likely just to fade gracefully into the woodwork.

First, Prescott tried to get the club to waive the rule, but the board was adamant about upholding this tradition. Whereupon, it was decided that he would have to go to Senator Smith and tell her that she could not receive an invitation. Smith hit the ceiling.

Facing not only her fury but also his own sense that it was justified, Prescott went back to the president of Burning Tree and did what he agreed he should have done in the first place. He told them, "Look, you *have* to waive this rule. It isn't going to hurt anybody. This has offended Senator Smith, I think with justification. We are talking about a United States senator, and I ask you to reverse your position." Eventually, the club agreed, but that didn't let Prescott off the hook yet.

As he told it later, "I went back to Margaret Smith, and I said,

'Margaret, I come to you now on my hands and knees, to your office, to say that I have gotten Burning Tree to reverse this decision and I beg you to attend.'

But she wasn't having any of it. She said, 'You couldn't pay me to go. Armed guards couldn't make me go!'"

Prescott did his best to make peace. "Now, Margaret, let's be reasonable. I am going to come for you in my own car and take you out there. I am going to drive you home. During the dinner you are going to be seated on the right hand of the president of the United States, and he knows that you are going to be seated there because I told him so."

Prescott admitted later that he hadn't really told that to the president, but he was trying anything he could to appease the angry senator. She did tell him she'd think it over, and after some time she did agree to attend.

Looking back, Prescott said his relationship with Margaret Chase Smith was strained for the next three or four years. "I was very much embarrassed about it," he said. "I really blamed myself for having been so foolish as not to insist in the first place that they waive the rule. But I was inexperienced and unsure about such protocols. I'm a great believer in the laws and abiding by rules, and I didn't insist on it."

Located at Bethesda, Maryland, just outside the nation's capital, Burning Tree was designed in 1924 by Alister Mackenzie. It was only four years earlier that the Nineteenth Amendment had given women the right to vote. It was definitely a man's world into which women were slowly making inroads. In fact, fifty years later Burning Tree, along with other prominent golf clubs, still does not allow women to become members.

Margaret Chase Smith and other pioneer political ladies were, no doubt, far more concerned about many other issues than chasing a dimpled ball around the countryside. When Hattie Wyatt Caraway, of Arkansas, was elected to the Senate in 1932, her new colleagues contained their shock by pretending she did not exist.

On the fairway or in the well of the Senate, Prescott Bush was one of the few who stood against this exclusionary tradition. And it seemed only appropriate that his son, then President George Bush, would present Margaret Chase Smith with the Presidential Medal of Freedom in 1989.

Prescott knew he was the particular target of Smith's wrath because, besides having made the mistake in the first place, he was the messenger of the bad news. And though he managed to resolve the matter about the dinner, tensions between the two remained for some time.

Life did become a bit more interesting when, in 1956, he was appointed to the Armed Services Committee, of which she was also a member. Their desks were next to each other on the Senate floor for several years. Finally, they got to the point where they could laugh about the invitation issue, and when he announced his retirement in 1962, she made what he described as "one of the most charming speeches in the Senate about me. At such times many are made, as is the custom, but hers was a beauty. So it shows that time is a great healer."

For Prescott the dinner situation illustrated well the political blind spot in Eisenhower that frustrated him. "Even a little thing like a dinner helped, you see, to bring him into contact with people who wanted to serve him, some of whom he had never met before that night. This helped pull the senators together in friendship for the president."

Eisenhower continued to have problems in the Senate because of this blind spot, particularly after the Republicans lost control after the midterm elections. One example was the Senate turning down Eisenhower's nomination of Lewis Strauss as secretary of commerce.

According to Prescott, "The Senate turned him down and not because Strauss wasn't a good man. It was purely political. Margaret Chase Smith voted with the Democrats, and that was a terrible disappointment to Ike. But everyone felt that her adverse vote was prompted by her resentment over his failure to sign her pet bill, which would have equalized the pay scales between the shipyards in New Hampshire, adjacent to her state, and in Massachusetts, where the two big government yards were."

But Eisenhower gradually began to get along better with his own party, helping him to gain some significant domestic successes. One was passage of the reorganization bill that established the Department of Health, Education, and Welfare. Another Eisenhower accomplishment was creation of the St. Lawrence Seaway, which for the first time enabled oceangoing vessels to travel from the Atlantic, down the St. Lawrence River between Canada and the United States, and directly into the Great Lakes. This proposal had been a controversial issue at the time. The inland senators had backed it because it would give international trade access to the heartland. New England legislators, however, were resistant, in part because they feared the seaway would harm their own part of the country. Prescott was among them, though later he was willing to admit he had been wrong. This time, however, the administration provided solid support and had a powerful man, George Humphrey, to work for the cause, and the measure passed.

Eisenhower appointed Oveta Culp Hobby—newspaper publisher, head of the WAC (Women's Army Corps) during World War II, and wife of a former Texas governor—to be the country's first cabinet officer as secretary of health, education, and welfare.

Prescott described Secretary Hobby as "a brilliant and beautiful woman [who] became a favorite of the president. She was very gracious and was very popular in administration circles."

They would develop a lasting friendship, one that echoed in the lives of the next generation. As Prescott described it, "We have a son in Texas, George, our second son, who moved there in 1946, right out of Yale. He went from Midland to Houston, and in 1964 he ran for the Senate against Ralph Yarborough. Mrs. Hobby's paper was very fair to him, in an area where the Democrats are predominant. Although she did not endorse him editorially, George felt the paper gave him a very fair break."

~≈~

By 1964 George Herbert Walker Bush had decided to run for the Senate against Ralph Yarborough—George's entrance into politics. He worked hard and waged a high-energy campaign, reaching out to voters of all persuasions, and he was genuinely surprised when he lost to his far more seasoned opponent. He took consolation in the fact that he had led the national ticket in Texas, collecting more than a million votes, but losing by a margin of three hundred thousand. The election was a family affair. Not only was it father George's first

Senate race, but it was the first political campaign in which son George W. was a part. His role was pretty basic—working on briefing books, looking up telephone numbers, and generally being a "gofer"—but nevertheless it would be quite the learning experience.

George W. traveled with the campaign entourage on a flatbed bus. Some of the time the bus passengers included the Black Mountain Boys, as well as the Bush Belles, pretty coeds in straw skimmers whose job it was to hand out brochures at each stop. The Bush campaign crew would pull into west Texas towns that were so small the city limit signs were back-to-back. The band would crank up, and candidate Bush would make a speech. It was old-fashioned, grassroots politics.

Lyndon Johnson buried Barry Goldwater in the 1964 election, and his coattails carried Yarborough to victory in the Texas senatorial race. George W. had taken time out of his first semester at Yale to fly down to Texas and watch the election results in a ballroom that had been rented for the occasion. He took his dad's loss hard, knowing how much it would have meant to everyone who loved his father for him to follow *his* father, Prescott Bush, into the U.S. Senate. By the end of the watch night, he sat by himself with his head turned toward a wall so people would not see him cry.

George had campaigned as an enthusiastic supporter of the senator from Arizona, who had electrified the Republican Convention in San Francisco with his fiery words, "Extremism in the defense of liberty is no vice; moderation in the pursuit of freedom is no virtue."

The still-youthful George, pictured in TV spots with his necktie loose and a coat slung over his shoulder, always on the move, did not ask his father to campaign for him and rarely invoked Prescott's name or his service in the Senate. He ran as his own man, battling

George and Barbara during his first campaign for Congress in 1966; he won.

the Democratic emphasis on his place of birth and fighting off conservative concerns that he was a "country club" Republican.

But in the defeat there were positive implications for the Bush family's renewed political ambitions. George was convinced he could get elected if he reached out to enough people, if they could hear his message.

The defeat reinforced the trait of the Bush men of losing the first time around. His father lost his first time in 1950 against William Benton, and later his son George W., lost to Democrat Kent Hance in 1978. Hance managed to turn the religious vote against him (not unlike the way Drew Pearson had wounded Prescott back in his 1950 run for the Senate!). In 1978 the George W. Bush campaign had run an ad in the Texas Tech campus newspaper for a rally in Lubbock. At the bottom of the ad appeared the notation, "Free Beer." To the Bush brothers—Neil had just graduated from Tulane and jumped into the fray—the blurb must have seemed a prudent if not essential reference. But the voters of west Texas soon found in their mailboxes a letter from a prominent Lubbock attorney who supported Kent Hance and was incensed by this invitation. "Dear Fellow Christians," read the opening volley, "Mr. Bush has used some of his vast sums of money to persuade young college students to vote for and support him by offering free alcohol to them. . . ."

"It was my first confrontation with cheap-shot politics," said George W. "It was smart because it obviously had an effect." He lost by six percentage points—not bad, all things considered. And he made himself a promise: "To never be out-Texaned again."

Two years later, in 1966, George ran for a House seat against an incumbent congressman and former district attorney, Frank Briscoe. This time he

George Bush, now an ex-oil man, goes to Washington.

resigned as chairman and CEO of Zapata Offshore and sold his stock, deciding that politics was a full-time job. He was not exactly bored with making money. When you have a family of seven, you can't afford to get bored. But as Aleene Smith, his secretary and an astute

Bush watcher, put it at the time, "His heart was no longer in making money." And this time George won the election.

He had followed almost to the letter the path mapped out by his father, Prescott, except that he made his money in Texas, not New York, and took the political plunge when he was fifteen years younger.

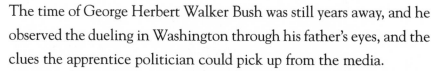

The time of George Herbert Walker Bush was still years away, and he observed the dueling in Washington through his father's eyes, and the clues the apprentice politician could pick up from the media.

On a distinctly personal level for Prescott Bush there were few more dramatic moments in the Eisenhower years than the confrontation with Taft in late April 1953. As the bureau chief for the New York *Herald Tribune*, Robert Donovan, wrote later: "Taft came as close to taking the roof off the White House as anyone ever has (except the president himself, coincidentally) during Eisenhower's tenancy."

The new congressman from the 7th District gets a kiss from Barbara in 1966.

The public learned in the 1970s that Ike had kept a meticulous and remarkably frank diary of those times. One entry, and one only, was marked "NOTES TOP SECRET. To be opened only at the direction of the president. One copy only of this memorandum made. Notes destroyed." This cryptic preface was initialed *ACW* by one of Eisenhower's secretaries, Ann Whitman.

The entry was dated May 1, 1953:

Yesterday was one of the worst days I have experienced since January 20 [his inauguration], the major part of the wear and tear coming through a meeting of the legislative leaders. Luckily, there were one or two features of the meeting that provided reason for a subsequent chuckle. All in all, therefore, the day's end was not quite as bad as some of the moments in its middle.

The difficulty arose at the weekly meeting of the executive department and the leaders of the Republican Party in the Congress. The purpose of the meeting was to bring about some kind of rough agreement as to the general character and extent of the changes that would be recommended by the administration in the Truman budget, submitted to the Congress at the end of the year.

After three months of sweat and study, the executive department had come up with a recommendation that the requests for new money be cut by something like eight billion, four hundred million. Moreover, the expenditure program for the fiscal year 1954, although largely frozen by commitments and contracts, made long ago, was cut and figured until it had been reduced by four billion, four hundred million.

This whole program was explained in the light of the desire of the administration to avoid any weakening of our defensive posture in the world; in fact, in the light of the need for increasing the presently available strength, particularly in the air forces.

Most of those present seemed to have a clear appreciation of the agony of the work and scheming that had gone into the business of making this kind of a cut. And it was carefully explained that future experience ought to bring about even greater opportunities for savings. Quite regularly, when we have achieved the defensive buildup that is considered the minimum necessary, savings should be much greater even if we have to continue in the conduct of the more or less "Cold War."

In spite of the apparent satisfaction of most of those present, Senator Taft broke out in a violent objection to everything that had been done. He used adjectives in describing the disappointment he felt that were anything but complimentary. He accused the Security Council of merely adopting the Truman strategy and, by a process of nicking here and chipping there, built up savings, which he classed as "puny." He predicted that acceptance by the Congress of any such program would ensure the decisive defeat of the Republican Party in 1954. He said that not only should he not support the program, but that he would have to go on public record as fighting and opposing it.

I think that anybody present was astonished at the demagogic nature of his tirade. Not once did he mention the security of the United States or the need for strength, either at home or among our allies. He simply wanted expenditures reduced, regardless.

The ludicrous part of the affair came about where several of my close friends around the table saw that my temper was getting a little out of hand. So, George Humphrey and Joe Dodge, in turn, jumped into the conversation as quickly as there was the slightest chance to interrupt and held the floor until I had cooled down somewhat. After that, I simply laid out the general basis of our global strategy . . . and the obvious truth that protection costs a mint of money. I defended the individuals on the Security Council, who had worked so long and so earnestly to bring about the projected savings. By this time that the senator had seen the reaction to his own talk, and heard the general comments about the table. Before the meeting was over, he had the appearance of being a jolly good fellow who had merely expressed himself emphatically.

Nevertheless, even assuming that he now accepts our position in complete detail (which I do not expect), he still has lost a great bit of his leadership in front of his associates who were here with him. I do not see how he can possibly expect over the long run to influence people, when he has no more control over his temper than seemed apparent at the meeting. Likewise, I do not see how he can maintain any reputation for considered judgment when he attempts to discuss weighty, serious, and even critical matters in such an ill-tempered and violent fashion.

Of course, I am pleased that I didn't add any fuel to the flames, even though it is possible that I *might* have done so except for the quick intervention of my devoted friends. If this thing ever has to be dragged out into the open, we at least have the right to stand firmly on the platform of taking no unnecessary chances with our country's safety, but at the same time doing everything we can to protect its solvency and its economic help.

Before the day was over, my friends dropped in to chat with me about the occurrence. (They) expressed the opinion that the whole incident cleared the air and enhanced the prestige of the administration because of the quite obvious acceptance by all the others present at the honesty and efficiency of our work.

The commotion soon subsided, which is not always the case. By the end of the month, Prescott Bush had arranged for Taft and Eisenhower to play golf. Unfortunately the senator did not play well and could not enjoy the company or the course. He was in the kind of back pain that will not allow you to straighten up.

The next day Taft checked into Walter Reed Hospital and shortly thereafter was transferred to another hospital in Cincinnati. Grim news soon reached Prescott Bush.

Eisenhower's tense and irregular contacts with Robert Taft had turned into what Ike described in his journals as "a curious sort of personal friendship," but a friendship, nevertheless. And Prescott Bush had helped make it so.

Barely a year away, a potentially more dangerous specter would threaten both parties and divide the nation, a cloud no larger than a man's fist, raised by a man named McCarthy.

8

⸺⊶⊷⊶⸺

Red Rover

No one could accuse Prescott Bush of being soft on Communism when, at the age of fifty-seven, he won in his third race for public office. (He had lost to his Democratic opponent by fewer than a thousand votes in his first run for the Senate. In his second try, he lost in the Republican primary.) In 1952 his biggest problem was finding a way to finesse the accusation that he was a capitalist, which he was, and worse, a Wall Street banker.

He was keenly aware of his newness to the arena when he learned that he and other candidates would be joined at a speakers' forum by none other than Joe McCarthy, the brooding Wisconsin senator and notorious hunter of Communists, real or imagined.

McCarthy had been anxious to speak in Bridgeport because Senator William Benton was running for reelection in the Democratic primary. McCarthy had been feuding with Benton on the Senate floor for some time. Benton had tried to have McCarthy expelled in 1951 on charges of fraud and deceit. In return, McCarthy had filed a two-million-dollar libel suit against him. Benton had waived his congressional immunity so the case could go to court, but McCarthy eventually dropped the suit. At the time of the primary, however, all this was still pending.

So McCarthy's supporters in Connecticut, largely a very right-wing group, hired Bridgeport's Kline Hall, the largest auditorium in southern Connecticut, and planned a political rally at which the various candidates could speak—and at which McCarthy could have a platform.

The Republican leadership, along with its candidates, held a secret meeting to decide if its men should participate. The committee split. Prescott was among those believing that they should not give McCarthy recognition by showing up. Finally, however, the decision was made to have the candidates appear, so Prescott was obligated to go.

As a proponent of civil liberties, Prescott did not fancy McCarthy's style, his attitude, or his bull-in-a-China-closet tactics. The Wisconsin senator was a blustery fellow who, detractors said, exaggerated his war record and, in his ardor to root out Commies, seemed to smear foe or friend for the sport of it. He was beefy and balding, with a perpetual five o'clock shadow and a voice that sounded like a phonograph record played at too slow a speed.

His biography was a politician's dream. Born on a dairy farm near Appleton, Wisconsin, in 1908, he was as Irish as Finian's rainbow. He was one of seven children of Timothy and Bridget McCarthy; three of his grandparents were born in Ireland, one in Germany.

At fourteen he dropped out of country school to work on his father's farm, and went broke raising chickens. Three years later, he went to work at a country store. He was nearly twenty-one when he started high school. In one year he finished a four-year program by carrying sixteen courses simultaneously. At Marquette, a Jesuit college in Milwaukee, he made the boxing team and switched from engineering to get a degree in law, which he received in 1935. Two years later, at twenty-nine, he became the youngest circuit court judge in the history of Wisconsin.

Even though judges were exempt from the draft, when the war came along, McCarthy, now thirty-three, enlisted in the Marine Corps, serving as an intelligence officer in the Pacific theater.

There were, of course, parts of his biography that he wouldn't advertise. He had won his judgeship through a campaign that included smearing the incumbent's reputation. Then he had drawn negative comment by granting quickie divorces to some political supporters, and he was censured by the state supreme court for destroying crucial evidence in a price-fixing case. And though he came home and campaigned as a war hero, it is not actually clear how much combat he saw other than, perhaps, as a photographer or passenger in a plane.

He later claimed to have been wounded while serving as a tailgunner, but the only wartime injury in the records was a broken foot incurred during a troopship hazing incident, when he fell down the stairs. Nevertheless, he once posed for a campaign photo at the tailgun turret of a plane, earning himself the nickname "Tailgunner Joe." It captured his self-image nicely.

In the 1946 Wisconsin Republican primary, he defeated Bob La Follette, son of former senator Robert La Follette, founder of the Progressive Party, and a three-term incumbent. The La Follettes, father and son, had represented Wisconsin in the Senate for forty years, and this was a huge upset. In the fall election McCarthy went on to an overwhelming victory after pounding his opponent with baseless allegations.

On his way to this victory, as in virtually all his races up to that point, he was accused of unethical conduct, but McCarthy was on his way to becoming a gigantic figure on the American political stage. So he would remain, even as he went down in flames.

Prescott Bush was apprehensive about their joint appearance, unsure though he was that Tailgunner Joe had ever heard of him. Of course McCarthy had. He knew the Wall Street part, knew Prescott's prodigious record of raising funds for the Republican Party in Connecticut, and knew that hardly anyone had an unkind word to say about him. McCarthy had often taken that kind of clean slate as a sign of weakness.

As he prepared for his appearance, Prescott also knew enough about McCarthy to inflict him with an uncharacteristic case of nerves. By this point McCarthy was the most newsworthy man in the Senate, thanks to his aggressive anti-Communist hearings, his speeches, and his personal attacks on the State Department. His targets included General George Marshall, the leading U.S. military planner in World War II and father of the Marshall Plan—which lifted heavily damaged Europe back on its feet after the war—and even President Eisenhower and his staff.

McCarthy also had wide public support in his Red-hunting, despite his scattershot attacks on well-respected figures. Yet, among those Prescott knew in Connecticut, many of the more moderate or liberal citizens not only disliked McCarthy, they feared him.

Fifty years later you must wonder, how could anyone paint Ike as a Communist pawn and still be walking around without restraints? And what kind of fruitcakes wanted to believe it? But this was the muddle of America in the middle of the twentieth century.

"In that post–World War II era," Prescott explained years later, "there was an obsession with this whole question of Communist infiltration. You had the Alger Hiss case, in which Nixon played a prominent part in exposing Hiss, an important adviser to President Roosevelt in the forties, as a Communist. This was the decision of the Congress, I believe, and Hiss was thoroughly discredited as a result of those investigations. The House Un-American Activities Committee had constant investigations going on.

"All this time, Joe McCarthy was waging a one-man campaign of his own and attaining tremendous publicity and nationwide recognition as the great fighter against the Red Peril. The Gallup Poll showed that about 52 percent of the people in the country approved of him, about 38 percent disapproved, and 10 percent were undecided. So this no doubt lent him considerable comfort in his 'crusade,' as he called it."

The evening was an unforgettable one for Prescott. When he and his party arrived, the auditorium was packed, with standing room only.

Prescott described the scene: "I never saw such a wild bunch of monkeys in any meeting that I ever attended. We were seated on the stage. Both Purtell and myself were invited to speak for a few minutes before McCarthy spoke. So our national committeeman gave Joe a rousing welcome to Connecticut, and the state chairman got up and did the same, and Purtell topped them both.

"And then came my turn. I walked to the podium with my knees shaking. I said that I was very glad to welcome a Republican senator to our state, and that we had many reasons to admire Joe McCarthy. In some ways, he was a very unusual man. Up to this point the crowd was fairly quiet. At least, I continued, he had done one very unusual thing—he had created a new word in the English language, which was 'McCarthyism.' With that, everybody screamed with delight.

"And I went on: 'But, I must say in all candor that some of us, while we admire his objectives in the fight against Communism, we have very considerable reservations concerning the methods which he sometimes employs.' And with that the roof nearly blew off with boos and hisses and catcalls and cries of 'Throw him out!' 'Go back to Russia.' 'Who the hell are you?' I finished my remarks with one or two innocuous sentences and sat down. They booed and screamed at me."

What happened next took Prescott completely by surprise: McCarthy got up, walked over and shook hands, and then invited him to dinner after the meeting. Stunned, Prescott agreed.

McCarthy then moved to the podium and spoke for about an hour—without notes, as Prescott later recalled—making an impassioned speech in which he damned Dean Acheson (Truman's secretary of state) and others. At one point, he held up a sheet of paper, waving it in the air, and declared that it held "the names of the one hundred Communists in the State Department." As Prescott observed later, this was a highlight of a typical McCarthy speech, and when he sat down the crowd roared with approval, rushing to the stage to shake hands with him.

After the meeting, Prescott, his campaign manager, the Republican state chairman, and McCarthy all went out to a popular local restaurant. At first, the others could only stand by while people crowded around to get McCarthy's autograph, but finally they were able to sit more quietly and talk.

McCarthy turned to Prescott and asked, "Now, Pres, what can I do for you? I want you to win this election."

Prescott replied, "Well, Senator, that's very kind of you. I'll tell you one thing you can do for me that would help me up here very much indeed, and that is if you would stop calling General Marshall a Communist."

McCarthy answered, "I never called him a Communist."

"Well, Senator, I have to differ with you. It's right in your book—the book you wrote. I have it." And Prescott named the page for him.

McCarthy didn't back down, though. "Now, listen," he said, "I didn't accuse of him of *being* a Communist. I said he was *either* a Communist or else he was stupid."

Prescott kept his voice quiet and friendly, but stuck to his guns. "Senator, you can't convince the people of this country that General Marshall is a Communist or that he is stupid. It only hurts us to have a great American idol assailed by you. After all, he led our forces through the war, and the Marshall Plan has helped rebuild Europe. He's a national hero. It hurts us to have a great Republican senator speak out as you do against him."

McCarthy was unimpressed, however. Then, after the group had discussed some other matters of interest, he asked Prescott, "Do you need any money?"

Prescott didn't want to accept money from McCarthy, so he told him, "A candidate usually needs money, but we're in pretty good shape up here."

McCarthy wasn't put off, however. He said, "Would you like me to send you five thousand dollars?"

Prescott, being diplomatic, replied, "Let me think about that, Senator. I think perhaps there are other candidates that need it more than I do. We're really in pretty good shape as far as our campaign finances are concerned."

Large amounts of money moved through McCarthy's office, most of it from wealthy supporters in the oil and cactus belt, eager to be counted. Prescott would not accept McCarthy's offer and risk having his opinions compromised.

Tailgunner Joe easily won reelection in Wisconsin, and Prescott Bush defeated Ribicoff by thirty-one thousand votes, thanks in no small part to the length of Eisenhower's coattails. Prescott and Joe McCarthy would see each other in the private dining room reserved for Republican senators, and these meetings were cordial. As Prescott said later, "He was very friendly. Nearly everybody liked Joe personally, even though many were offended by his behavior on the platform and on the Senate floor.

The Army-McCarthy hearings began in 1954 and were a major national event. On opening day, April 22, the Senate Caucus Room was packed, and an estimated forty million people watched on television. Two basic questions were on the table: (1) Had McCarthy and his aide, Roy Cohn, exerted improper pressure on the U.S. Army to gain preferential treatment for a onetime McCarthy staff member, David Schine, who had been drafted the year before; and (2) Had the army used Schine as a "hostage" to block McCarthy's investigation of the supposed "Communist influence" in the army? Beyond that, however—giving even greater importance to the

Prescott hits the campaign trail on a brisk Connecticut day.

hearings—were basic constitutional questions about the separation of powers and about domestic subversion, and even the question of McCarthy's own future.

Part of the background to these hearings was McCarthy's role as chairman of the Senate Committee on Government Operations and its subcommittee on investigations. In that capacity, he had carried on his "crusade" against Communist infiltration of our government by charging that the army was also "infested." McCarthy had given an especially hard time to Secretary of the Army Bob Stevens, whom Prescott counted as a good friend.

"We were very much provoked with his behavior," Bush reported, "and that of his two principal assistants, young Roy Cohn and G. David Schine. They really were obnoxious." McCarthy had picked

Cohn as the chief counsel for his subcommittee. Schine had the grand-sounding, but unsalaried, title of chief consultant in psychological warfare.

The senator made a ghastly mistake when he sent the pair on an eighteen-day tour of American military bases in Europe. One of their tasks was to determine if books promoting Communism were being read by our troops. Army sources began sending home reports on the activities of the "two junketeering gumshoes."

Traveling to Paris as a member of the Randall Commission—appointed to study U. S. economic policy with respect to foreign trade—Prescott Bush joined Senator Harry Byrd, of Virginia, for lunch at the Supreme Headquarters of the Allied Command in Europe.

(Although born in West Virginia, Byrd was unrelated to that state's Robert Byrd, another Senate icon who would later serve more than forty years. Harry moved to the Old Dominion state when he was a boy.)

"After lunch," Prescott said, "I was walking out with General Norstad, the deputy commander. I asked him, 'General, we hear back home that the behavior of Mr. Cohn and Mr. Schine in Europe has been really damaging to the interests of the United States. Do you think that's true?'

"He said, 'It was so bad that it can't possibly be exaggerated.'"

In November 1953 Schine himself was drafted into the army. Cohn swung into action to arrange a posting for his friend near New York State. A limousine fetched him for his weekend passes and returned him after their reunions. Cohn badgered various generals to give Schine, who was called up as a private, an immediate commission. If his friend wound up going overseas, the army brass now charged, the fast-talking young lawyer vowed to "wreck the army."

McCarthy and the army were now pointed toward a collision that would be historic. In January 1954 the army had called up a New Jersey dentist named Irving Peress. Because dentists routinely received ranks equal to their professional experience, Peress was immediately made a major.

When Peress refused to answer all the questions on a loyalty oath, he asked for and received a discharge. In fact, the army had already decided to issue one after its own investigation.

McCarthy filled the air with his cries of, "Who promoted Peress?" He demanded punishment for the nonexistent culprits and a court martial for Peress himself. The senator was clearly not satisfied when told that, since the dentist had left the service, he could hardly be recalled.

McCarthy was brutal in his treatment of General Zwicker, the commanding officer at Fort Monmouth, who testified he had no grounds to order a court-martial. McCarthy told Zwicker, a hero of the D-Day invasion of Normandy, that he was unworthy of his uniform.

This time McCarthy's words and deeds were met with ridicule. After all those months of investigation, noted Senator Ralph Flanders of Vermont, all he had found was one "pink army dentist."

Now that the army had gone on the attack and accused McCarthy of exerting improper pressure on behalf of Schine, it was poetic justice that the senator did not even like the playboy with the wavy blond hair. He tolerated him as a friend of Roy Cohn, apparently unaware of the kind of ribald gossip that the pair's association had generated and that would surface indirectly in the hearings.

The army versus Joe McCarthy was the second big spectacle coming to television, the medium Prescott Bush had first heard about
when he helped finance CBS. Despite its critics and the small, grainy
pictures that were common then, television had found an outlet in the
fifties for its unique capacity to entertain, inform, and educate at the
same time. Two separate political forums provided the ideal theater.

The first, in May 1950, had been the Senate Crime Committee
hearings, which catapulted the committee chairman, Estes Kefauver
of Tennessee, to national prominence. The hearings were held in six
major cities, with a parade of characters out of Damon Runyon tes-
tifying while millions watched.

In New York the star witness was gangland's elder statesman, Frank
Costello. Forbidden to show his face during his testimony, the cameras dwelled on Costello's writhing hands, which frequently cradled
an English Oval cigarette. The grateful manufacturers, ecstatic over
such a windfall of publicity, shipped him large quantities of their
product each month, which Costello would forward to Veterans
Administration hospitals.

Then came McCarthy, the army, and thirty-eight episodes of one
of the most dramatic confrontations ever seen outside a courtroom.
Prescott took it all in from a seat near the front of the room. He
would later observe, "I would say that the lawyer from Boston helped
nail Joe's hide to the wall."

Joseph Welch, a courtly, white-haired fellow who favored bow
ties, had been appointed special counsel to defend the army. When
Welch learned that a young attorney in his firm had been a member of a legal guild once listed as pro-Communist, he advised the
McCarthy side that he was sending the young man home rather than

make him an issue in the case. But in the last week of the hearings, McCarthy could not resist using the information. Although totally irrelevant to the point then under debate, he rose to accuse Welch of harboring in his firm "a young man named Fisher who has been serving the Communist cause."

As McCarthy droned on the rumpled Bostonian rose at his seat and cried out, "Let us not assassinate this lad further, Senator. You have done enough. Have you no decency, sir, at long last? Have you left no sense of decency?"

The galleries applauded the honest indignation of Joseph Welch. And to millions looking on across the land, Joe McCarthy—smirking, whispering behind his hand to Roy Cohn—seemed coarse and irresponsible. This was the man who had accused the Democrats, under Franklin Roosevelt and Harry Truman, of "twenty years of treason." Truman dismissed the remark as the ravings of a "pathological character assassin."

When Eleanor Roosevelt and Edward R. Murrow, among other voices, blasted him as a menace to the American way of life, McCarthy recalled that as a boy he and his brother were assigned to kill the skunks that had invaded his mother's chicken yard. "The more success you have hunting skunks," he said, "the worse you smell."

As the TV crews began to pack up their cameras, Prescott Bush believed the McCarthy spell was soon to be broken. For one thing, the Wisconsin senator had never resolved the conflicting numbers he had been throwing out. Speaking to a women's club in West Virginia, he had initially used the figure of "205 card-carrying members." Then a few days later he had said 57, and on other occasions 100 or so.

Prescott Bush felt that if McCarthy actually had a list, he should have given it to the State Department or the FBI, but he never did. In addition, when questioned by the lawyers for the army, he took the Fifth Amendment several times—the very action for which he had denounced so many others.

Finally after several weeks of hearings, a motion was made in the Senate to condemn McCarthy for bringing the Senate into "dishonor and disrepute." At issue were not only his disregard for the rules of law and fairness but his vicious attacks on other senators.

Charges were combined into two counts, and a special, bipartisan committee was appointed to conduct hearings and then report back to the full Senate. Prescott was among the six members.

As Prescott described the hearings: "The chairman was Arthur Watkins, of Utah, a Republican. Joe called him 'cowardly' and 'stupid.' He made an unforgivable attack on Bob Hendrickson, a Republican from New Jersey. Called him a 'living miracle, a man with no brains or guts.'"

Before the hearings were completed, the 1954 midterm election campaign was in full swing, so action on the special committee's report was deferred until after the November election. Two weeks after the election the Senate went back into session for the sole purpose of acting on the Watkins Committee report.

Each of the committee members made a statement. As Prescott would recall later, only two of the three Republicans supported the committee's report, which supported censure of McCarthy. Prescott was one of them, making his statement on the Senate floor and seeing it go into the record. And when the whole Senate voted, McCarthy was censured by a vote of sixty-seven to two.

In his quiet way, Prescott Bush had been smoldering for months. He believed that the White House had been embarrassed by one man willing to spread fear and distrust with no regard for the consequences. McCarthy had been on the nation's front pages for four years.

The State Department had agreed to clear its appointments with him.

The president had not disagreed with him in public, even after he called George Marshall, Eisenhower's great friend, "an instrument of the Soviet conspiracy."

One symbolic act, one well-aimed gesture, one final flap of the cape was needed to remove the bull from the ring.

Prescott had made an engagement to play golf with the president before going back to Connecticut, and it was scheduled for the day after the Senate's special session. Then, as luck would have it, that morning it rained and the golf date had to be called off. Prescott thought he might have caught a break because talking politics with Eisenhower, while he played golf, was poor form. And this was a conversation that needed to happen—that or something equivalent.

As he considered how to approach Eisenhower, on one front Prescott had no doubts. He knew McCarthy did not intimidate the president, despite his silence through so much. After all, this was the man who had gone toe-to-toe with a couple of the strongest, most hardheaded and aggressive characters of the age, U.S. General George Patton and British Field Marshal Montgomery. But Eisenhower's advisers had convinced him that if he took on McCarthy, it might only serve to force the Republican senators to rally behind their colleague from Wisconsin. In fact, that happened anyway, to some extent. On the other hand, McCarthy had been slashing away across all lines.

So, with the golf date canceled, Prescott called Eisenhower's assistant, Sherman Adams. After making a point or two, Prescott pressed his suggestion.

"Sherm, Arthur Watkins, the chairman of the joint committee, has taken a terrible beating on the censure vote. McCarthy called him a coward on the Senate floor. He's a wonderful man and doesn't deserve that. I think it would be appropriate if the president sent for him and gave him a good pat on the back for doing an unpleasant job well and with courage."

Adams proved quite open to this suggestion, and replied, simply, "Will do."

President Eisenhower, with Prescott Bush at his side, signs the Federal Highway Act of 1956.

Before noon that very day, the president had invited the Utah senator to the Oval Office and praised him. A few minutes later, Watkins stood beside Eisenhower's press secretary, Jim Hagerty, and told newsmen that the president had congratulated him on "the very splendid job" he did as chairman of the special committee and said that he had "performed a great service to his country."

Prescott and Dorothy were in their car, driving back to Connecticut in the rain that afternoon, when they heard Watkin's statement on the radio and then an hour later McCarthy's reply.

The Wisconsin senator was completely unrepentant. "There has been considerable talk about an apology to the Senate for my fight against Communism," he said. "I feel rather that I should apologize to the American people for what was an unintentional deception upon them. During the [1952] campaign, I spoke from coast to coast promising the voters that, if they would elect the Eisenhower administration, they could be assured of a vigorous, forceful fight against Communists in government. Unfortunately, in this I was mistaken.

"I find that the president, in one breath, congratulates the senators who hold up our work and, in the next breath, urges patience and tolerance to those who are torturing American uniformed men."

The reference was to eleven airmen imprisoned by Red China. Eisenhower had expressed his outrage, but counseled against letting the United States be goaded into war by Red Chinese acts. He specifically rejected a blockade of Communist China, a response advocated by McCarthy.

(Nearly half a century later, another American president, George W. Bush, would be confronted with the challenge of obtaining the release of an Air Force crew whose plane had been forced down over China. Diplomacy, and a carefully crafted apology, gained their freedom—and the return of the aircraft.)

In the days after McCarthy's barbed remarks were carried on network radio, a firestorm of reaction engulfed "Tailgunner Joe."

General James A. Van Fleet, the retired commander of the Eighth Army in Korea, made public a telegram he had sent: "In the past, I have supported you in your fight against international Communism but never have agreed with your methods. This last attack on our great president causes me to withdraw all support."

What shocked the Grand Old Party was McCarthy's personal attack on Eisenhower, referring to him directly. In the past McCarthy had sharply criticized the administration, but had softened these assaults with kind words for the president. Now he had gone beyond the pale. Even two of his most prominent supporters in the Senate, Karl Mundt and Bill Knowland, had to disavow McCarthy's statement.

So this was, effectively, the end of Joe McCarthy. He had gone so far beyond any limits of propriety that his best friends had deserted him. And he never knew that Prescott had engineered Watkin's congratulatory meeting with the president that had led McCarthy to his one last excess.

Within a few weeks, Eisenhower gleefully passed on the latest change in the Washington vocabulary: "Do you know what they call McCarthyism now? McCarthy-wasm."

Prescott did have some lingering concern. He had been warned by party leadership not to vote against McCarthy in the censure move because it would "kill him" in his 1956 campaign. He had ignored the advice and spoken out because he thought it was important for the country and the right thing to do.

Nevertheless when he went back to Connecticut in early December after the historic Senate vote, he wondered what he might find.

"When I traveled around the state, appearing before the League of Women Voters and other groups, I was very curious about how much hostility I would encounter. Instead, I was amazed at the number of people who came up to me and thanked me for my vote on Joe's censure. I found that many people felt very deeply that he had become a dangerous man."

Outside a handful of smaller newspapers, the press was also favorable to Bush—and negative on his colleague Bill Purcell, who had defended McCarthy.

Later Prescott would remark about the famous, and infamous, senator, "He was a very strange fellow—a Dr. Jekyll and Mr. Hyde, if you will. He had a very warm personality. The elevator man and the guards and staff around the Capitol, they all loved him. He was nice to everybody. He had a very easy way with people. He was, in a sense, an attractive person. He was witty and amusing, and the blue-collar workers loved him because he was a big wheel who noticed them and spoke to them.

"I didn't think he was really a mean fellow, at all. I think he only did mean things when he thought it would help his case or attract attention. I think he gloried in the press that he created. He reveled in the publicity that became his; his picture on the front page of *Time* magazine."

Prescott had wondered why the media seemed to do so little for so long to counteract the McCarthy bandwagon. Yet, one night he had dinner with Jim Linen, then president of Time, Inc., and Linen asked him why the Senate hadn't done something earlier about McCarthy.

Prescott pointed out that it was pretty hard to "reel him in," when *Time* put him on the cover and devoted as many as four pages to the issue of the day, telling their readers how powerful McCarthy was. Linen was amused by the exchange.

Among the nonelected elite, Henry Luce and his weekly news-magazine ranked near the top of any ranking of opinion shapers. The print media, led by the *New York Times*, the *Washington Post* and the *Chicago Tribune*, and the radio networks were most Americans received the news. The thunder of television's hoofbeats were still a half-decade away, with only 35 percent of the country wired in 1956.

McCarthy cast his spell best in person, in front of large and partisan crowds. He was overbearing on radio and, even worse, boring on TV.

Prescott learned more about this complicated figure from his secretary, Margaret Hampton, who had worked with McCarthy for a couple of years. While she disapproved of what he was doing, she said he had always been nice to his staff and called them all by their first names.

She recalled how McCarthy was a horseracing fan and loved to go to the track in Bowie, Maryland. He would tell her he was going out to the Bethesda Naval Hospital, and she knew he meant he was going to the races. In 1953, McCarthy had married a former member of his staff, Jean Kerr, who had been a beauty contest winner at George Washington University.

"Everyone who worked for him liked him," said Prescott. "He was likable. But not all of us thought he was truly sincere about his witch-hunting. I didn't think he could have been because so much of the information that he referred to as 'facts' were not facts at all, and he must have known that. He was not stupid. He was bright. But Joe was a gambler, and he would gamble with the truth if it served his purpose. He didn't mind doing that any more than he minded gambling on the races or the stock market."

Whatever Prescott thought of McCarthy, he knew that he had attracted great support from the public. "Money poured in to Joe McCarthy from all over the country," Prescott would recall, "envelopes with cash, one hundred dollars, ten, five, and notes that said, 'Dear Senator, I'm with you. Spend this money in your crusade the best way you think.'" Prescott estimated that McCarthy had received tens of thousands of dollars in the mail every month when he was making all these speeches. He never allowed any investigation of his finances, but always had money and was a free spender.

In February 1955 the fervent McCarthyites in Connecticut decided to honor him with a testimonial dinner, and once again, the occasion was a sell-out. More than four hundred people attended.

A pensive Prescott at his desk with a photo of Dotty at his elbow.

Prescott, looking toward his 1956 campaign, braced himself for the royal attack that McCarthy would unleash as a reprisal for his having voted and spoken against him. Prescott learned later, to his amazement, that McCarthy never even mentioned his name. Instead, he gave what Prescott saw as "a typical McCarthy speech," and every time he mentioned Eisenhower, the crowd booed—proving, as Prescott said, "that the U.S. always has been blessed with its share of *gassy diehards*."

There was a poignant conclusion to the curious relationship between the patrician Bush and the earthy McCarthy.

As Prescott described it later, "In the spring Joe's health began to fail. He had developed a terrible drinking problem and was intoxicated a good deal of the time. Even back in 1953, Bob Stevens told me he went to Joe's house one morning in New York, privately, to talk with him off the record about the hearings.

"The first thing Joe did was go to the sideboard and pour himself a big glass of whiskey—at ten o'clock in the morning. So there was no doubt that alcohol had a lot to do with his death.

"On the first of May, in 1957, he was in Bethesda Naval Hospital, and I went out there for a physical examination. It turned out that I was on the same floor as McCarthy.

"There was nothing fancy about it. I had a very simple little room. I was paying my way. We all did. We didn't go there for free. When I had finished my exam and was dismissed, I walked down the corridor toward the elevators. On my way I passed Joe's room. There was a nurse standing there, and I said, 'I'm Senator Bush of Connecticut. I wonder if I could see Senator McCarthy for a moment, just to wish him well.'

"She said, 'Oh, no, Senator, he is much too ill for that. He is much to ill to have visitors.'

"I said, 'Well, would you take a little note to him?' Oh, yes, she could do that. So I wrote out a friendly little note, hoping that he would recover soon and be back with us. By the time I reached the Senate Office Building, a telephone message was waiting for me that Joe had dictated, in which he thanked me warmly for coming to see him and [saying] how much that courtesy meant to him.

"The next day he died, and I suppose I was the last senator to have any contact with him."

Joseph Raymond McCarthy died on May 2, 1957. He was forty-eight years old.

This same courtesy and respect would later be exhibited by Prescott's grandson at Lee Atwater's bedside. In March 1990 the family learned that Atwater, strategist on George Bush's 1988 presidential campaign and family friend, had an inoperable brain tumor. He was only thirty-nine, and he and his wife, Sally, were expecting a baby in a month.

In Lee's final days, the younger George flew to Washington to be at his bedside and read passages to him from the Bible.

<hr />

The hardened political observer may find these death scenes maudlin, but Prescott Bush set an example for compassion. Whether you bury a friend or foe, even in politics, you can find charity and empathy for life's early endings.

It was through his acts of kindess and principle that Prescott maintained his popularity in his state and beyond. Lanny Davis, Yale's Class of '67, the Clinton counselor, was the son of a die-hard liberal. When Lanny told his father that George W. Bush was a class behind him, his father responded, "Prescott Bush! A fine man. Even though he is a Republican, he stood up to Joe McCarthy."

When the first George Bush stopped by the Yale campus to visit his son, Lanny Davis told him, "My father was a great admirer of your father."

9

———⚬⚬⚬———

Alfalfa Party

$\mathcal{I}$n the realm of pop culture, the theory has been frequently heard that girls eventually grow up to become their mothers, and boys turn into their fathers.

Prescott Bush Jr. believes that he has been a witness to this very evolution. "I don't believe George realizes how much like our dad he has become," said the older brother. "One of Dad's favorite things was to sit up in bed, or on a couch, chewing on an unlit cigar, with his sons gathered around him. And as they talked, sometimes all at once, he would nod and go, 'Uh-hmmm.' George does the same thing."

From the third generation, a voice out of Florida weighs in with a similar observation. "What I remember most clearly about my grandfather," said Jeb Bush, "besides how disciplined he was, is the fact that all his children were in awe of him. And it is pretty much that way with our dad, although he let us joke around with him, even as kids. I don't think Gambs did that."

There is an unusual family dynamic at work here, with George

147

Herbert Walker Bush holding the funnel. Prescott's core values and attitudes passed through him, and to his own children, with adjustments. The rules were a little lighter, the humor much more elastic.

The story that most clearly defined the generation gap was the one that took place at the country club in Greenwich, on a day when George was invited to play golf with his father. Prescott stormed out of the clubhouse after a friend of his told an off-color joke, announcing gruffly, "I don't ever want to hear that kind of language in here again," and leaving his son, then about fourteen, sitting in front of his locker.

"I didn't know what to do," says George. "I finally got up and followed him out. But I really didn't think the joke was all that bad. My brothers and I had a much higher tolerance for jokes that were somewhat bawdy. Dad had a good sense of humor. Ours tended to be saltier."

But nearly all the Bushes, of whatever era, had a teasing wit and a willingness to be the brunt of their own jokes. To listen to the banter, to see the playfulness, was to get a sense of how fiercely close they have been as a family, in ways the public rarely sees.

On a breezy summer day at the compound in Kennebunkport, surrounded by all the children except George W., who was busy elsewhere, Barbara explained over a light lunch the parental pecking order: "The truth is, all five children are much closer to their father because he is a much more selfless person. I'm the mean one, I'm the tough one, and I have to be because he's so sweet. They don't want to let him down."

In one loud chorus, all the kids yelped and one or two made a gagging motion with their thumbs and Doro said, "Aww, Mom, you're laying it on a little thick!"

George taking his daughter Doro for a sleigh ride in the snow.

And quietly, in a reasonable tone of voice, the forty-first president of the United States interrupted. "Hey," he said, "she's entitled to her opinion."

George W. is, or was, the one with the wildy irreverent sense of humor. Once he became president himself, his position no doubt imposed restraints on him that did not apply earlier, such as the time the Bushes entertained Queen Elizabeth at a White House luncheon. Barbara placed George W. at the end of the table, as far from Her Highness as possible.

He was then in his oil drilling phase, had stopped drinking, but still on occasion had a wad of chewing tobacco in his cheek and wore cowboy boots. "He's the black sheep of the family," Mrs. Bush said in a state whisper to her royal guest.

"Is that so, George?" asked the queen. "Are you the black sheep?"

"Yes, ma'am," he replied. "I guess that's so. They say every family has one."

It is uncanny how often these experiences repeated themselves, in one form or another. A year or two earlier, the president and first lady had paid an official visit to Buckingham Palace. The Bushes happened to pass the royal gift table, and their attention was diverted by an interesting sterling silver bowl with three tiny feet. George looked up and asked what it was. The queen replied, "I don't know. *You* gave it to me."

A royal evening: President Bush and Barbara entertain Queen Elizabeth and Prince Philip. According to Burkes Perrage, the Bushes are descended from British royalty.

The funny stories by or about the first George often have been unintentional. The press needled him for weeks after he explained a loss in the Iowa straw polls by saying, "A lot of the people that support me, they were off at the air show, or their daughters' coming-out parties, or teeing up at the golf course for that all-important last round." No one considered that he might have been poking fun at an image the media had been so quick to seize upon.

In his day, Prescott Bush had a very deft hand at a dry one-liners, usually inner-directed. In 1962 when the Cuban missile crisis had left the country in a state of heightened nervousness, a neighbor asked him if he planned to build a bomb shelter. The prevailing scientific opinion then was that a family would need provisions and resources for three months to allow the contaminated air to clear.

Prescott paused and arched his caterpillar eyebrows. "Let's see," he said. "I would be cooped up with Dotty, our kids, and their kids for ninety days in one room. I think I would rather play golf in the fallout."

It was possible in his time to serve ten years in the Senate and to be deeply respected by your colleagues yet be little known outside your own state. The access, the instant exposure, simply wasn't there, unless you were running for president. There are not many books devoted to senatorial wit.

As it happens, intensive research reveals that Prescott Bush did, after all, have a flirtation with the office his son and grandson would later occupy. Although not widely advertised, even at the time, a third party nominated him in 1959 for president—the Alfalfa Party.

While Bush was a serious and even formal politician, who mediated antagonisms within his own party, and opposed the witch hunts of the day, he possessed a sly wit and was not reluctant to poke fun at himself.

Much like the Gridiron Dinner, the Alfalfa Club's annual mock convention crossed all political and power lines and was meant to be good, clean fun. The nominating process was conducted in the same spirit as the later campaigns of the comedian Pat Paulsen, one of the stars of the television show *Laugh-In*.

Paulsen's platform once included a plea for everyone to "join the war on poverty. Throw a hand grenade at a beggar." But appearing on *Laugh-In* was a serious opportunity for politicians of the time. Richard Nixon, trying to soften his image for his 1968 comeback, did so and recited one of the show's trademark lines, "Sock it to me."

But even as a gag, the compliment to the tall, patrician senator from the country's third smallest state was implicit. He was ideal for the role because he had a spotless reputation, exuded an air of dignity, had the respect of his peers and opponents, and did not object to turning a joke at his own expense.

Stuart Symington, the senator from Missouri, placed his name in nomination, and he was escorted to the podium by a wedge of other Democrats. The group consisted of two more senators, Harry Byrd of Virginia and Richard B. Russell of Georgia; former cabinet officers John Snyder, Charles Sawyer, John Sullivan, and Tom Clark; and Democrat Leslie Whiffle, the former secretary of the Senate. At the Alfalfa Club jokes about bipartisan support tended to be a bit heavy-handed.

Prescott was introduced to the dinner audience and the convention as the senior senator from Connecticut and president of the Whiffenpoof Club of Yale. And to the cheers and applause of the crowd, he began his speech, which showcased a humor not everyone knew he had:

I am deeply moved by your faith in me . . . and I give you my solemn pledge that I will not rest until this speech is over. . . .

For many years I was in private business, until one morning I awoke to the realization that all those years I had been working for myself. And it was with little reluctance that I gave up working for myself and came to Washington. Now others work for me. I can just enjoy it.

Of my staff I have demanded the same devotion to duty that I have shown. Indeed, everyone in my office shoots under eighty. Carrying on the great tradition of Thomas Jefferson, we have endeavored to prove the axiom that the government that governs best governs least.

Now, friends, I want to inject a very personal note. My decision to come to Washington was very difficult for Mrs. Bush. It faced her with the necessity of completely changing her way of life, giving up her home, her friends, and her family to come with me to Washington. Many of you will no doubt recall that now legendary statement I made at the time, when I said, 'I regret that I have but one wife to give for my country.'

Now, I ask you, why is it that some people seem reluctant to accept the possibility that politicians are public-spirited folks? I have heard politicians referred to as being in good spirits, or even full of spirits, but rarely public-spirited. I think Rudyard Kipling, in his immortal poem "If," explained it very well when he wrote:

> If you can keep your office when all about you
> are losing theirs and blaming it on you,
> You're a politician, my friend.

It is my belief, my whole belief, that public office is a sacred trust. This reminds me to say right now that contributions for my campaign can be mailed to my trust, at the Guaranty Trust Company.

Now, the subject will naturally arise as to my running mate, and I *urge the convention to withhold any rash decisions until I myself have had a chance to talk with some of the more likely candidates. I recall here the immortal words of the late Grantland Rice, when he wrote:*

> *The rules of life apply the same*
> *To any sport you choose.*
> *It matters not how you play the game,*
> *So long as you never lose.*

It is with that thought in mind that I propose a new possibility for the vice presidential nomination. Inasmuch as the incumbent president of the United States (Eisenhower) is not eligible to run for that high office, might he not be a suitable running mate for me? Of course, it might be desirable to withhold any decision until the next Gallup Poll is released. I don't want any stone around my neck.

[For the balance of his speech, Prescott literally broke into song, offering his message to a tune from the Broadway hit, *The Music Man*: (Prescott Jr. said that his father saw the movie version of *The Music Man* five or six times "because he so enjoyed the scenes with the barbershop quartet."

And he continued:

Next, I want to talk about something serious, like taxes. So let us talk about taxes, my friends. I mean, the money that we have to pay. I don't see why a guy like me should dissipate his means, when it doesn't mean beans. I suggest instead that we borrow the money that we need from some foreign land, that we borrow the money, why sure! Now, who, I inquire, is the obvious choice to bear upon their backs our income tax, but the Soviet Union? Of course.

Why sure, you say, we'll let those fellows in the Kremlin pay, by requesting a loan with so much interest that they couldn't refuse. No, they wouldn't refuse because they wouldn't want to lose all that interest. And . . . when the notes come due, we would tell them we were short a billion or two, and they wouldn't dare attack us. . . .

Now the time has come when reluctantly I must leave this platform and move out into the great campaign that lies ahead. I guarantee to you that I am inadequate for this task. As the strains of our new campaign song fill the hall, I emphasize to you that harmony must be our guidepost—harmony in our party, harmony of purpose, harmony of ideals— and I pledge myself, my friends, and my family to the task of making the most out of our victory! (Applause, cries of "more!")

At this point, jokes aside, he noted that he had been asked to sing the Whiffenpoof Song that night, in recognition of the society's fiftieth anniversary. And in his rich, soothing bass, Prescott Bush led the crowd in singing the classic lyrics, a sample of which is reproduced here:

From the tables down at Mory's to the place where Louis dwells,
To the dear old Temple bar we love so well,
Sing the Whiffenpoofs assembled with their glasses raised on high,
And the magic of their singing casts its spell. . . .

We are poor little lambs who have lost our way,
Bah, bah, bah . . .

We are little black sheep who have gone astray,
Bah, bah, bah.

With that, Prescott Bush returned to his seat, and Senator Stuart Symington concluded the program, declaring, "Gentlemen of the convention, you have just heard the greatest acceptance speech for president of the United States of any candidate, of any party, in all of recorded history. All that remains is for each of us to hold aloft our blazing banner and go forward to victory. . . .

"The president of the Musicians Union and the director of the Armed Forces Band shall be the joint chairmen of our national committee. Instead of facts, we shall offer song and story. Our battle cry shall be, 'Baritones for Bush.'"

10

∙∞∞∙

The End of Camelot

The sixties were a time of change. There was a sexual revolution brewing, a rise of feminism, a call to the protection of civil rights, and a strong demonstration of antiwar sentiment. It was a crossroads for the American culture. This included a change in politics.

A true, full-contact election was looming in 1960, but compared to more recent engagements this one seemed almost polite.

In certain contexts we may be loath to repeat the suggestive old phrase that politics makes for strange bedfellows. But the thing is, Prescott Bush liked Jack Kennedy, really enjoyed him—a feeling close to fondness—even though they were from different religions, meaning one was a Democrat and the other a Republican, as well as belonging to different churches.

Kennedy had the capacity to surprise you in a good and gentle way, unlike Dick Nixon, his perpetual rival—at least in the minds of those who remember the 1960s. Nixon tried, heaven knows, as when he tried to cozy up to David Frost during their television interviews, to be a regular guy, by casually asking the British import off-camera, "Did you do any fornicating over the weekend?"

Prescott remembered standing on the Senate floor one day in 1959, a time when Jack's baby brother, Ted Kennedy, was a junior in the University of Virginia law school.

"Jack came up to me and said, 'Would you like to do me a favor?'

"And I said, 'Well, what would that be?'

"He said, 'My brother Teddy is going to be made president of the Law School Forum at Charlottesville, and he wanted me to get you to come down to address their annual meeting, when he's going to be inducted.'

"I said, 'Why in the world does he want me?'

"'Well,' he said, 'they want a Republican. They've had two Democrats lately, and they want a Republican.'"

You pause to think about the compliment Kennedy paid the senator from Connecticut. Time is running out on the decade of the 1950s, the Eisenhower Years, and everyone knows John F. Kennedy intends to seek the Democratic presidential nomination. The economy is slipping. Fidel Castro has rolled out of the hills to overthrow the Batista regime in Cuba. The Cold War is raging and the Russian satellite called Sputnik is still orbiting the earth with that eerie, Mickey Mouse beep. And here are these two tall, distinctive New Englanders huddled on the floor of the U.S. Senate, causing no telling how many heads to swivel.

Prescott said, "'Jack, I'm not looking for speaking engagements in Virginia right now, but if you'd like me to do it, I'll do it.' So I did. I went down, and Teddy met me at the airport, and we had a lovely evening. I spoke, and he was inducted, then we went out to his house afterward.

"He had a home on the edge of Charlottesville, and he had about twenty young people out there. I remember I stood in front of his fireplace while they fired questions at me for about an hour. We had a wonderful time.

"Then, the next year, 1960, he's a senior. He graduates and immediately gets into the campaign with his brother. Two years later, he takes Jack's seat in the Senate. It's fantastic, isn't it? That's moving."

In 1960 Prescott stumped across Connecticut for Nixon, and into Pennsylvania and Delaware. He tried mightily to keep his heart in it, but that wasn't always easy. In some ways he identified more closely with Kennedy's positions—on welfare and civil rights, taking care of the dispossessed. He was disturbed, even mystified, by the campaign Nixon ran. Why didn't he reach out sooner, or more forcefully, to the president he had served for eight years? Ike remained the invisible man of the 1960 election until almost the final days.

There was no meanness, no pettiness in Prescott Bush, but if he had been the candidate, he would not have allowed Kennedy to get away with what he felt were gross distortions of the foreign policy record.

"I was very much annoyed with Kennedy," he said, "when he took the position that our respect around the world was diminishing and that we were

Prescott Bush adjusts the hat of vice presidential candidate Richard Nixon in 1960.

losing the goodwill of the free world because our foreign policy was inadequate.

"I did not think this was true and believed it was purely a campaign tactic. But it seemed to me to be unfair that he should demean the president and take this dim view of our effectiveness in foreign affairs. I think our prestige has slipped steadily since the Eisenhower administration went out, and it strikes me that we were at a low ebb in world approval under the Democrats, before and after Ike.

"It is probably true that our relations with Russia were at a low point, but that isn't saying much. When Khrushchev banged his shoe on the table at the U.N., were we supposed to feel inferior? Some believe Nixon was hurt by the U-2 incident and our pilot [Francis Gary Powers] being tried and imprisoned over there. But it also showed that we had military assets no one had even imagined— a plane that for a year or more had been flying over enemy territory so high it was undetected.

"I think we have to credit the Eisenhower administration with a relatively successful experience in foreign policy, during years that were very difficult. Many difficult issues raised their ugly heads, such as the Suez Canal matter, when the British, French, and Israelis grabbed the Canal. Eisenhower pressured them into withdrawing, and that was a decision with high peril."

These were our friends, and Egypt had, after all, the means to disrupt international shipping. During an election, candidates often do not let the facts get in the way of an outlandish statement, and the only test is whether the claim is believed. This is part of the game, but Prescott Bush never felt that foreign policy should be treated as a sport.

"It made the British very angry," he noted, "and the French, too. I'm not sure that de Gaulle's present antipathy to the United States may not still have behind it some of the resentment that was felt by the French at that time. But even so, in that particular case, the United Nations as a whole was with us."

In an election decided by one hundred thousand votes, the analysts could cite a wide range of reasons for Nixon's defeat: his sickly pallor during the first debate, compared to a tanned and vigorous Kennedy; the sluggish economy; JFK's ability to create the perception of a "missile gap." Prescott believed the outcome was most influenced by the "Eisenhower factor."

"It's hard for me to believe that Nixon didn't encourage him to work for him more aggressively, but it is possible that Nixon did not. If that was the case, Nixon made a terrible mistake. Knowing the two of them, Dick may have hoped he could win without having to feel Ike had carried him. And Ike may have felt that Nixon was ignoring him a little too much and got his back up a bit. He's a little touchy, like all of us are at times.

"I heard it said at the time that Ike was annoyed that he had not been asked to play a bigger part in the campaign. Nor did I feel that Nixon did a very effective job of defending the Eisenhower record in the debates. Of course, no one hears much about the substance of the debates. Nixon's appearance was a distraction. Kennedy looked neat and trim and attractive, and was very sharp and precise in the arguments.

"Nixon made a very weak showing. Not only did Kennedy come off the best with his general conduct overall, but he showed for the first time, to the nation, that he had real forensic ability. He was a fine debater, and you could not shake him. Looking at them, I thought, 'If I were judging this on debating points, as you do in high school or college, I would have had to vote for Kennedy, apart from Nixon's unshaven-looking appearance.'

"So that got the vice president off to a poor start early in the campaign. Subsequently he did much better in the other two debates. He improved in each one. But Kennedy, off to a flying start, was sort of able to hold this advantage.

"Jack handled the religion issue extremely well. His Catholic faith was supposed to handicap him. He handled that with a good deal of dexterity. He went down to Houston and let all these Baptist ministers confront him, and he convinced them that if he were elected, the Catholic Church would not impose its beliefs on him; he would be his own president, and so forth. It was a very bold and courageous move, and he did it well.

"So all the time he is growing, in the estimation of the people, from the picture of this candidate who looked so young at the convention in California, the night he made his acceptance speech. His stature is increasing all during the campaign, and I don't think Nixon made any gains in this respect. Nixon's image—I always disliked that word, but you have to use it sometimes—was more favorable during his years as vice president than it was during the month of October 1960."

Within the context of his world, which was at bottom a political world, Prescott Bush was always circumspect and often generous in his observations about the Kennedys. The same can be said of his son George, who ran his first race for the Senate the year after the assassination, and who has known Ted for nearly forty years. The Bush men have had their critics, but they have not been hated or hateful; they do not polarize large groups or incite hysteria.

But the Bushes are competitive, and they know, even if they do not acknowledge it, that they always will be compared to the Kennedys. How can they not? Both families, so attractive, so proud and loyal, so filled with tribal love for one another. Whatever their convictions, whatever side of the line they stand on, they have been willing to pay the price for the ideal of public service.

Prescott admired John F. Kennedy as a certified war hero, as he was qualified to do; his son George had been shot down twice as a navy pilot; the second time he had been plucked from a raft by a submarine just off the shore of a Japanese island.

Prescott Jr. shook his head over the Kennedy myths, the stamina of the many keepers of the Kennedy flame. "Why do people find them so fascinating?" he asks. "So many embarrassing things about old Joe Kennedy, and the brothers. All those women, the actresses, Marilyn Monroe, the Mafia girlfriend [Judith Exner], all the stories. *Agggh*. But no family has suffered more, and I guess that is part of it, the mystique."

He has answered his own question.

Bobby Kennedy once said of Jack, "At least half of the days he spent on this earth were days of intense physical pain."

To many, JFK came to represent a turning point in American life. "President Kennedy's grandmother was living in Boston when he was assassinated," said Bobby. "She was also alive the year President Lincoln was shot. We are a young country."

It is a cruel and dreadful toll, one that no family should have to bear: the first brother, Joe, lost over the English Channel in the last weeks of the war; John and Bobby; Jackie and JFK Junior, all gone, early. And earlier.

Prescott Bush knew that when people mourned the Kennedys, they were mourning for so much lost potential, for the dry, self-mocking humor of a president who governed for a thousand days. From the senator, the two Presidents Bush inherited a belief in elevating people, not belittling them.

Prescott was not glad that his candidate lost, but he was not depressed when he attended the inauguration. He had campaigned for Nixon in three states—Connecticut, Pennsylvania, and Ohio. Kennedy carried them all. There might have been an inside joke in that, but none came to mind.

"The day before the swearing in," he reminisced in later years, "there was a terrible snowstorm in Washington. The city was just under a blanket of snow, about eight inches, and traffic was tied up. It was a terrible mess.

"But the day of the inauguration, it was clear and sunny, although very cold—below freezing. In the wind and cold, Robert Frost had a problem reading his poetry. Still, it was a very impressive occasion. Kennedy, hatless, made a splendid appearance and gave, I thought, a high-level speech, with the wonderful line, 'Ask not what your country can do for you, but what you can do for your country.' Which is about as high as you can get in philosophy, in my judgment. It was all very well done.

"That night he came to a meeting of the Alfalfa Club, which is this organization in Washington made up of political figures and people in the professions and business and the military. There was a dinner of about six hundred that night. Jack was a member; so were

Lyndon Johnson and a lot of senators—Joe Martin, Charlie Halleck, and others. The main purpose of the club is to hold this one dinner, one night a year.

"The president speaks for about five minutes at the end of the dinner. Kennedy gave a very amusing, witty speech. This was when he said, 'You know, I've been criticized for naming my brother to be the attorney general of the United States. But I don't see why a man shouldn't have an opportunity to learn something about the law before he goes into private practice.' This rather brought down the house, and he defused the nepotism issue by making light of this very serious charge against him.

"The Democrats went all out, with grand parties and a lot of movie stars and Frank Sinatra. They did it Hollywood style. I thought it was overdone, myself, but the people who watched on television were entertained by it.

"I had a moment with Jack at the Alfalfa Club dinner, and I told him I thought he gave a first-class speech. And it was. It would bear rereading any day.

"In the time he had, he made a real effort to implement the themes he had touched on. One of the early projects was the Peace Corps, which I felt favorably about, enough to become one of the Republicans who agreed to cosponsor the bill in the Senate. I put my name on it. I did that after quite a long talk in my office with Sargent Shriver, the new president's brother-in-law, who was to be appointed as the first director of the Peace Corps. After Shriver described to me just the way it would work, I thought it was a very economical approach to creating goodwill. It looked to me like a much cheaper way to do this than through the big economic-aid programs, which were compounding our balance-of-payments problem, creating a deficit there. So I supported it. I believe the Peace Corps has been worthwhile for us and should be carried on."

Prescott and the new occupant of the White House had a few shared visions, among them arms control. He liked the move Kennedy had made, appointing Jack McCloy to head this effort. McCloy had been assistant secretary of war under Henry Stimson, had been high commissioner of the Allied occupation in West Germany, and president of the World Bank. He was not a partisan guy, and Prescott had confidence in him. If anyone could persuade Congress to pass a disarmament bill, Jack McCloy could.

"The point was," said Bush, "that while we are arming to deter aggression, we should look forward to a time when we may not have to do so much. At the least, we should be planning how to bring about a disarmament program between the great powers. While it is sort of paradoxical, as our military budget is going up astronomically, here we are pushing for a rollback in the arms race.

"We sent a fine man, Bill Foster, to Switzerland to meet with the Russians, and they sat around and had a very interesting time. Just what they put on paper and signed, I don't think anybody could tell you. But Bill is a patient man with a lot of energy. He's a Republican who served in the Truman administration, as undersecretary of commerce when Averell Harriman was the secretary.

"What had to impress you was the way Kennedy picked the best fellows he could possibly find to tackle this assignment. Jack McCloy testified before the Foreign Relations Committee and talked with individual senators, convincing them this was worth doing.

"I was one of them. Later I had McCloy on one of my television

166

shows in Connecticut, and we discussed the reduction of arms on the air for ten minutes. I support that effort, and I thought it was a smart move politically for Kennedy. He did not want to be perceived as a warrior president. Here he shows everybody that what he really wants is to work toward disarmament."

~⊰~

Prescott did not achieve the high office his son and grandson did, and the journalists and historians of his day did not record his hand in legislation or his influence on events. This was more a reflection of the low profile he seemed to prefer than the neglect of the chattering classes. He set for his family, and others, a standard of good manners and the value of informed thought. The quiet of his presence was like the silence of a forest, where the lack of noise does not indicate a lack of life.

In retrospect, it is a pity he was not more assertive and his actions more closely observed. What a waste that his wisdom, and the precision of his commentary, and his influence on his presidential blood, are only now being rediscovered.

He correctly foretold the open wound that would bedevil every president since Eisenhower, an island ninety miles from Miami—Castro's Cuba. More than forty years later, we have not found a way to free the Cuban people, although we have liberated several of their better baseball players. We still have not found a solution to a threat we can no longer identify. Our policy toward Cuba is based on the theory that if we wait long enough, Fidel will eventually die.

Prescott Bush remarked, "There was a plan developed by the

CIA over a period of six to eight months, and if it had been followed, I believe our Cuba problem would have been over right there. Eisenhower had not decided whether to give the invasion a green light, and it was handed off to Kennedy, who made the decision not to have air cover or to involve American troops. He wanted it to appear that these Cuban exiles, with little or no help from us, were landing at the Bay of Pigs and invading the island to overthrow Castro. This was in April 1961.

"I was and still am a great admirer of Allen Dulles, who was the director of the Central Intelligence Agency. My feeling then was, if the plan had not been changed, if the U.S. forces had cooperated to the extent that they were counted on to do, the invasion might well have succeeded. One can't ever be sure about that. Certainly, the CIA is a very thorough organization, and I don't think it would have undertaken an enterprise of that kind unless they had all kind of assurances that it was going to work.

"Once we decided not to have anything to do with it, not to give them airpower and so forth, it placed the invading Cubans at the mercy of ground fire from the Castro troops on the beach, and it was, of course, a fiasco. This was generally how it was described and what it was—a fiasco. It hurt Kennedy and was really a reflection on his judgment, in my opinion. There were different views expressed in the White House, at that time, but the decision was his alone. He took the blame completely on himself for the failure at the Bay of Pigs and moved on, and in doing so won back some respect.

"I wasn't one of those who had doubts about the CIA being responsible for this sort of undertaking. For many reasons, military and economic, I believe we need to know what is going on within the countries that do not wish us well. I was in Mexico City right after the 1960 election and had a briefing by a CIA representative. We had a small corps there, very small. They knew the Russians had a complement of 158 agents in their embassy, with a big stone wall around it, guards at the entrance, nobody ever admitted inside. But they were 158 strong, doing propaganda and intelligence work for the Russian government, and that was just in Mexico City. All through Latin America, the Russians had this type of operation.

"Whether the CIA should be limited to gathering intelligence, or involved in a military action, I think would depend on what is necessary. If the intent is to bring about a counterrevolution in Cuba, throw Castro out, and give the people a chance to have a decent democratic government, I would be in favor of that. There has to be planning. There has to be secrecy. There has to be an underground movement, as we had in both World Wars, in Europe, and a great many lives were saved. But how you use the CIA is what the British call a 'dicey' question.

"We had the eventual freeing of the Cuban prisoners through a sort of barter arrangement, medical and humanitarian supplies in return for the prisoners. There was popular support for it, but I am not sure that judgment was sound, either.

"Then, in October 1962, Senator Kenneth Keating of New York received information from reliable sources that the Russians were in the process of shipping missiles to Cuba, and these installations were being made. In my experience, it was not unusual for persons within the military who were troubled by a situation to leak information to a senator.

"Photographs taken by our high-flying U-2 pilots confirmed this, pictures of the missile sites, and this naturally alarmed the administration. Kennedy flew back from a trip to the West Coast and made a speech on national television, declaring that the Russians had lied and violated an agreement by installing missiles that were offensive and could strike most of our major cities, and demanding that they be taken out. He mobilized the navy and blockaded Cuba. After a very tense week or so, of high-stakes diplomacy, several Eastern bloc ships bound for Cuba changed course, and they began to disassemble the missiles and load them onto Russian ships. The famous line at the time was, 'We were eyeball to eyeball, and they just blinked.'

"We had pictures of these great big boxes being loaded onto the decks of the transport ships, but I was disappointed we did not board the ships and make sure that was what they were removing. Time seems to support the assumption that they were taken out, but I never thought we had the proof we should have had for such an important decision. I was not satisfied that the navy had made a careful enough examination of what was going out of Cuba."

There would not be another crisis to compare with the Cuban missile confrontation until, one might argue, the Persian Gulf War and, ten years later, the terrorist attacks on the World Trade Center and the Pentagon. We didn't know it back then, but the Cold War was winding down and Communism would cease to be seen as America's most serious threat.

During the sixties, when Prescott was nearing the end of his political run, his son George was beginning his career in Texas, and his grandson George W. was on the academic path—Andover to Yale to Harvard Business.

The irrepressible younger George arrived in Andover, Massachusetts, in the autumn of 1961, as a new student at the prestigious Phillips Academy. This was a whole new ball game for the confident kid from Texas, as he would soon discover. Education is important to the Bush family, and when it came to their children, they spared no expense.

This was his introduction to "the halls of ivy." He and his father had

A family portrait: George and Barbara with Neil, Jeb, and George W standing. Doro and Marvin are in front.

visited the campus a few months earlier so he could get a look at it. George W. had no strong feelings either way about coming here, but he sensed that it was important to his parents that he attend this school and then Yale just as his father and grandfather had before him.

He would not given his soul to Andover and Yale as his father and grandfather had done. He had been put off by what he regarded as the eastern snobbishness, the liberal bent of the campuses, and the misery of having devout Republican roots in a time when the country wallowed in the Watergate scandal.

Phillips Academy, just twenty-five miles north of Boston, was founded during the American Revolution by Samuel Phillips Jr. Paul Revere had designed its seal, and John Hancock, a delegate to the Constitutional Convention, had signed its Act of Incorporation. In 1789, George Washington, who had nephews attending the school, visited and spoke to the student body assembled on the lawn.

Phillips Academy prides itself on being the oldest such school in the country and goes by "Phillips Andover," or even just "Andover," to differentiate itself from the unrelated "newer" school in Exeter, New Hampshire, that bears the same name. (Phillips Exeter was only founded *after* the Revolution.)

This was a place of cold winters, formal ideas, and no girls—it was the first time George W. had been to an all-boys school. It was very different from the twenty-five-year-old coed private schools of Texas. The tradition and discipline of Andover were a culture shock that required adjustment.

Retracing the paths of his father and grandfather, he immediately went out for sports, although with something less than their success. He played varsity baseball and sat on the bench in basketball next to Clay Johnson, his friend from Fort Worth. He did one season of junior varsity football and then was elected head cheerleader, which meant he spoke at assembly.

The academic load was harder than anything he had encountered before, and it did cut into his socializing. Clay Johnson, a fellow Texan and later a member of his political staff, recalled, "We were in way over our heads in a foreign land. We had to struggle just to catch up. There was an article in *Time* magazine our first or second year. The headmaster of Andover was on the cover. I remember reading that and thinking, *Oh, my God, we're at the hardest school in the country.*"

Struggle though it may have been, during his last year at Andover, George W. and his roommate, John Kidde, were appointed proctors for the tenth grade. And the faculty did not award this responsibility to those who just slid by academically.

It was during his second year, in October 1962, when the Soviet Union tried setting up ballistic missiles on Cuba and President Kennedy responded in a face-off now known as the Cuban missile crisis. Then, during George W.'s senior year, President John F. Kennedy was killed before the country's eyes by an unseen assassin while visiting Dallas. Television brought us the funeral, and everyone saw the veiled young widow and her beautiful children watching the procession, tiny "John-John" saluting as his father's casket came by.

Community memorial services were held in churches and auditoriums across the land, bringing together citizens of almost every political stripe. November 22, 1963, became one of those events about which people for years asked, "Do you remember where you were when . . . ?" Much as a stricken nation would do later, following September 11, 2001.

At midyear—after Lyndon B. Johnson had taken charge in the White House, and life was getting at least somewhat back to normal—George W.'s parents gave him a copy of Barry Goldwater's book *The Conscience of a Conservative*. The Bush family supported Goldwater in the 1964 election, and they wanted their first son to know where the senator from Arizona stood. The deepest participation in politics George W. had done while at Andover was getting elected cheerleader, but he did read the book, and he liked most of what he read. Goldwater's story was part of the Bush story, too, and the whole picture offered another kind of political education. When Goldwater beat out New York's Nelson Rockefeller for the Republican nomination in 1964, his impassioned, even militant, conservative philosophy brought out the beast in those on the fringe, notably the John Birch Society.

The media called them kooks, but they were active and well organized, and it wasn't just the presidential race they targeted. George W.'s father, running for public office for the first time, the U.S. Senate, at that, should have lifted the spirits of every Republican. But in 1964, with early polls showing Goldwater ahead of President Kennedy in Texas, the hard right still viewed George Bush with suspicion—a Texas oilman with manners and a heart and a country club membership.

While all this was going on, of course, George W. was still a student. Now he was putting on a stretch drive to raise his grades because it was time to interview with the dean about college choices.

He made it clear that he intended to go to Yale. It was in large part the reason for his presence at Andover. And, in truth, he had been born a Yalie. Nevertheless he was ambivalent. His grandfather

Prescott Bush, whose career at Yale was legendary—along with his later devotion—said, "George, Yale is not a choice; it is a commitment. Do you know what that means?"

"I think so, Senator," said the grandson (the boys were always expected to call him Senator). "It means sticking with something no matter what."

Prescott pointed to the young man's breakfast plate. "It is the difference," he said, "between ham and eggs. The chicken is involved. The pig is committed."

At Andover, the dean took a less Talmudic view of the decision facing young George W. He suggested, tactfully, that the youth should list two other choices. So George W. wrote down, "(1) Yale, (2) Yale, (3) Yale."

Yale became his mission, not because he believed he had an obligation to his family but because he had a resistance to people telling him what he was incapable of doing. However (to be historically honest), he did, as a backup, apply to the University of Texas as well.

On the day the college responses came in, all the seniors marched over to their post office boxes. There they shared their jubilation over getting the "good," skinny one and not the "bad," fat one (returning the applicant's supporting documents). Thirty-eight percent of Andover's senior class would be moving on to New Haven. Perhaps only the dean at Andover was more shocked than George W., when he learned that he would be among them. He had received a "good envelope"—Yale's acceptance letter.

The indoctrination at Yale felt familiar. The first day was all confusion and nervous energy and everyone asking directions. George

W. just circulated, shook hands, and said, "Hi, I'm George Bush." You would be surprised how many people one can meet that way.

George W. had come to Yale during a relatively quiet transition time—before the war in Vietnam escalated, the cities and campuses erupted, or the assassinations of Martin Luther King Jr. and Robert Kennedy occurred. Although the times were changing, at Yale the good life was still fraternity life. George W. was elected president of the Dekes, and Roland Betts was the chairman. Together they ran the fraternity and so were responsible for whatever was going on.

Mostly, parties were what was going on. Friday and Saturday nights were social, with music, dancing, drinking, and fun. Every Deke showed up for the dances, and those who were not members hustled to get tickets. George W. would hire Ike and Tina Turner or Kool and the Gang, for maybe five thousand dollars, and they'd be on the band-stand the whole night. Crowds of two to three hundred fought to get to the dance floor, and the rest wandered through the frat house.

However enthusiastically involved in social activities George W. might have been, or even guilty of the occasional misdeed, the product of Midland's public schools was not casual about getting an education, even though he didn't always toe the line. Despite some people's ear-lier doubts, he did do what was necessary to graduate, and eventually he went on to earn an M.B.A. at the Harvard School of Business.

It was while he was at Harvard that the Vietnam War officially ended and Richard Nixon was scandalized in his second term in office. Before George W. graduated from Harvard, Nixon resigned from the office of president of the United States.

In his assessment of Richard Milhous Nixon, George W.'s grand-father, the thoughtful, soft-spoken Senator Prescott Bush, was blunt and uncompromising. He said Nixon reminded him of Winston Churchill's description of Russia: "A riddle wrapped in a mystery inside an enigma."

Prescott respected the intellect and drive of the native and most famous product of Whittier, California, who once confided that his ambition as a young man was to become a sportswriter. He would live to see Nixon stage two national comebacks and win the White House, but not quite long enough to see him entangled in the Watergate scandals. Prescott died in October 1972, three months after five men were arrested for breaking into the offices of the Democratic National Committee.

"I never had a harsh word with Nixon," he said, "but he had in him a streak of mendacity. He was not a man you could feel comfortable with on short acquaintance. He was surely one of the most complicated political figures of my time.

"I suppose I knew Nixon better than most of the Republican senators because I played golf with him, frequently, at the Burning Tree Club. You get to know a fellow's character on the golf course. I would ride with him in his big Cadillac, which the vice president enjoyed, and we talked going out and coming in, but I never felt really close to him.

"He had only one friend that he really trusted with his confidence, and that was Bill Rogers, the attorney general the last three years under Eisenhower. I'm sure Rogers was the only one Dick confided in, his innermost fears and hopes and so forth, and maybe that is a good thing for a man in high public office, not to have too many close friends. But I don't really believe that. I believe a man is strengthened by having friends he can confide in and with whom he can talk freely and frankly.

"Certainly, a man of the background of Dick Nixon should be discriminating enough to know whether he could trust a person or not. But he was very, very cautious about trusting anyone. When Ike suffered his heart attack in Denver, it placed Nixon in an awkward position. Should he attempt to assume the duties of the president or not? He consulted with only one person, and that was Bill Rogers. He never gave the appearance of one who was exercising the president's authority, and I respected him for his handling of that crisis."

No one outside his closest circle ever knew that Prescott Bush was among a handful of Republicans who made a clandestine effort to have Nixon removed from the ticket before Eisenhower ran for reelection in 1956.

In 1955 terrible floods had caused havoc in most of New England, and Prescott traveled to New Hampshire in the autumn of that year to attend a meeting dealing with flood control legislation. He used the opportunity to schedule a private meeting with the governor of Massachusetts, Christian Herter.

"There was considerable discontent about Nixon," he said, "especially in the more liberal wing of the Republican Party. Much of this had to do with the McCarthy era, when Nixon avoided taking a position even when the Senate was in session discussing McCarthy's behavior. I asked him if he would make even one statement about it, and he refused. He would not commit himself. Even after McCarthy directed a fierce attack against President Eisenhower, Nixon remained mute.

"He had gained his first national attention, one might recall, as a Red-hunter in California. He won his seat in Congress by labeling the incumbent, Helen Gahagan Douglas—a charming lady, a former actress, and the wife of actor Melvyn Douglas—as a 'pinko.' He flayed her with charges of Communist associations, and the liberal press resented it very much. The reputation he acquired in that 1950 campaign hung over him throughout his career.

"Later, as a member of the House Un-American Activities Committee, he had a prominent role in the Alger Hiss case. So he apparently felt he could not criticize McCarthy.

"I asked Herter whether he would be interested in running for the vice presidency in '56, if Ike decided to make a change. He was non-committal, more negative than otherwise, but he did not rule out that possibility.

"Two or three weeks before the convention, in California, I met with Sherman Adams, who was still the chief of staff. There had been increasing talk about nominating Christian Herter as a rival to Nixon. But when I raised that prospect with Adams, he snapped, 'Listen, just forget about Herter or anyone else. Nixon is going to be the president's choice.'

"That was the end of that, and any revolt against Nixon was shut off somewhat abruptly. Eisenhower then made a noticeable attempt to upgrade his usefulness, sending him around on different missions—including to Russia, where he had the famous 'kitchen debate' with Khrushchev.

"Unhappily, in the campaign of 1960 the president was asked a question during a press conference about whether Nixon had been helpful in the formation of any policies. He answered to the effect of, 'Give me a week, and I'll try to think of one.' This was a very damaging remark, and I believe Ike felt the question was a reflection on his ability to form his own opinion on important policies, and he reacted in a moment of temper. I'm sure he regretted that. But it demeaned Nixon and hurt him badly.

"He could have parried it by saying, 'The vice president has always been helpful to me in connection with these matters.' With Kennedy winning by less than 1 percent, an incident of that kind may have been decisive. That response contrasts sharply with the way Eisenhower stood by him when the charges of a Nixon slush fund surfaced early in the 1952 campaign. I personally thought Dick gave a masterful performance, for a man of his youth and lack of experience, going on national television and facing the nation."

The viewers gave Nixon an overwhelming endorsement. Eisenhower praised his candor and said the people had spoken. Nixon had not directly addressed the charges, but he made his case when he noted that his wife, Pat, did not even own a fur coat, only a "good Republican cloth coat." And, he added, they had received one gift they would not give back, a black cocker spaniel named Checkers. He had saved his spot on the ticket with what became known as "the Checkers speech."

And the very competent Christian Herter would be heard from again. When John Foster Dulles died of cancer in May 1959, Herter, then one of his deputies, was named to succeed him as secretary of state. Dulles had defined the art of brinkmanship as diplomacy stopping just short of going to war. Herter could not match him in presence or personality, and he was by then suffering from acute arthritis.

"He did his job well," observed Prescott Bush, "in the brief time he was there, and got along well with the president and Congress. But he was walking on crutches and had difficulty standing for periods of time. He took quantities of Bufferin or aspirin every day.

Wherever he found himself, he was looking for a seat, and this relieved his pain, which was severe."

In a final irony it was Richard Nixon who persuaded George Bush to run for the Senate again in 1970, giving up a safe seat in the House and opposing the far-left liberal whom even Lyndon Johnson despised, Ralph Yarborough. This was truly a race George could win just by being himself, running slightly to the right of Costa Rica.

Barbara and George W. support the candidate on election night 1970. He lost his senate bid to Lloyd Bentsen.

But a weird thing happened on the way to the Senate. Yarborough lost in the Democratic primary to Lloyd Bentsen, another oilman, former congressman, former war hero, and a bona fide conservative. The whole party swung behind him, LBJ and John Connally and all of the Rio Grande Valley, where the Bentsen family had been a force for years. Bush was in a box. He couldn't move left, and there wasn't enough room on the right to hook slide around his opponent.

When the election was over, Nixon offered George the post of ambassador to the United Nations in 1971. He gladly accepted because, "You don't say no to your president." He did this even though the assignment would encourage his critics on the far right, who believed that the U.N. was a modern Tower of Babel, where the Communist bloc and emerging nations sent their diplomats to gang up on America.

An intent Ambassador Bush listens to the translation of a speech at the United Nations.

George himself had made the world body an issue in his campaign for the U.S. Senate in 1964. "If they admit Red China," he said, "we ought to pull out." This was a theme advocated by his party's presidential candidate, Barry Goldwater.

But now George literally had changed his viewpoint. From the window of his corner office, on the top floor of the U.S. mission offices, he commanded a panoramic view of the East River, but for most of each day he worked with his back to it, reading the files that were brought to him by the pound.

In his early months on the job, he was briefed, debriefed, and rebriefed. He read three scholarly books on the U.N., including Dean Acheson's biography, *Present at the Creation.*

"In that period," he recalled later, "I thought, The next guy who comes up to me and says, 'Here is a book you should read,' and hands me something with 650 pages and all kinds of ibids in the back, I might just hit him in the nose."

He and Barbara kept an apartment at the Waldorf Towers, but Barbara enjoyed her husband's office and the guest quarters connected to it. "That was a wonderful time for us," she said. "It was like being able to go to a World's Fair every day, except you could watch it from your window, or walk across the street."

The one sad note in what was otherwise an uplifting move was that George's father was in declining health. Yet this was just the kind of duty Prescott Bush had had in mind, important work with the potential to change lives, when he preached the gospel of public service.

George Bush believes that the United Nations can be what its designers hoped it would be, a monument to the pursuit of reason—whatever the best intentions of honorable men and women can make it. His opinion matters because he was there in the thick of the Cold War years.

He never fit the image of the old-school, morning-coat and top-hat kind of ambassador, of course. The protocols of high-level diplomacy never constrained him.

"I am sure," he said, "that the people around there wished that I had gotten bogged down in it a little more. They were not used to Texas informality. I don't mean you went up to the secretary general and clapped him on the back. But if you knew people well enough, you could set protocol aside and just relax and be human beings."

He found out quickly that diplomacy was not exactly the gentleman's game of fencing, where one had time to hand one's coat to a second. During his first week on the job a cease-fire in the Middle East had been broken, and he was whisked to a series of Four Power talks, sitting opposite men who had been on the job for thirty years. These were the kind of meetings where press releases are never issued. No one knows what was decided, but the world did not go up in a great, orange ball of flame.

George had watched the suave Henry Cabot Lodge, and then the sardonic Adlai Stevenson, rise to defend the United States against Russia's propaganda assaults, doing it with eloquence. Now it was his turn to defend our virtue and policies.

He brought to the task obvious assets: He was educated, sincere, persuasive, able to process large volumes of names and information.

Jeb Bush campaigns for the GOP ticket in 1988 with Maureen Reagan, future presidential daughter.

He was also a handsome six-footer with a good tennis game. True, he had carried these qualities through a recent Senate race in Texas and lost. But look at it this way: He had lost a state and gained a planet.

"Personal goals were secondary to me at that point," he said. "There is a feeling of trying to accomplish something for your country, all the idealistic things that each of us has beating in our hearts. . . . One day I was shown a photograph of a witch doctor in Africa, with shells around his neck and sticking pins in a doll. This was the way they tried to cure smallpox. In 1970 the U.N. went in there and in six months all but wiped it out. That is a darned exciting story, whether you lived in a village in Kenya or in Levelland, Texas."

George went from being ambassador to the U.N. to serving as chairman of the Republican National Committee just as Watergate was unfolding. After that, under Gerald Ford, he went to Beijing, China, to head up the U.S. Liaison Office there, and then returned to the U.S. to become director of the Central Intelligence Agency.

Any of these jobs might have disqualified a person of ordinary will from even thinking about running again for high elective office. But in 1980 Ronald Reagan invited George, who had been his leading rival in the primaries, to join his ticket as the nominee for vice president.

They governed together through Reagan's two terms in the White House. Then, in 1988, Bush moved his own desk into the Oval Office.

The other jobs—the U.N., China, the CIA—he considered part of paying his dues. He was the son, after all, of a senator who had been a town meeting moderator for seventeen years.

A point probably needs to be made here, and George W. made

one. You could write lyrics to it, so familiar is the refrain: "There is no Bush dynasty, not now, not ever. The Bushes don't think that way. To talk about a political dynasty would be an act of conceit. And I am quite sure that these sentiments reflect the feelings of the late Senator Prescott Bush, former President George Bush, and Governor Jeb Bush of Florida, as well as Governor Bush of Texas, our first ladies, kids, and pets."

Early on, in the private family councils, John Ellis (Jeb) Bush, the second son, was considered the likely heir to the family political tradition. He was the studious, gentle, more serious one. Jeb liked keeping up with the issues of the day, and took an interest in how policy was shaped, how the sausage was made.

Physically, he was taller and heftier than George W., with the dark hair and sweet round face that came from his mother's side, the Pierces. Jeb was earnest. The night of the almost infamous confrontation between the elder George and his first son, it was Jeb who stepped in to relieve the tension. Of course, the incident became a favorite of anyone intrigued by what George W. called the "psuedo-psychological-me-and-my-dad stories."

Home on a holiday from Yale, young George had taken his fifteen-year-old brother Marvin out drinking, and when they returned home he drove over the neighbor's garbage cans, creating the kind of disturbance one might associate with the landing of an alien spaceship.

Mom and Dad were still awake, reading in bed, and word was sent to George W. that his father wanted to see him. As he stood in the doorway, weaving slightly, the defiant young man uttered the immortal words, "Do you want to go *mano a mano*, right here?"

"That was Jim Beam talking," said Barbara. "His father never said anything. He just looked up from whatever he was reading, and looked over his glasses at him, and young George just withered."

It was at this exact moment that Jeb broke in, with the news that George had been accepted to Harvard Business School. He had told no one that he had even applied. "I don't know if I'm going," he said airily. "I just wanted to show that I could do it."

Jeb had size and strength—he could hit a baseball over houses— but he did not appear to have the intensity and charm of George W., who hadn't quite figured out what to do with them.

This time Jeb Bush has the funny line; dad and big brother share a laugh.

Not burdened by the name, Jeb never felt he was competing with his dad's record, or had an obligation to meet certain expectations. Yet he was the one who didn't travel the road most taken. He graduated from the University of Texas, moved to Florida to work in real estate, and spent some time in Venezuela as a banker. But he never hesitated to drop what he was doing to work on one of his father's campaigns. He was the most conservative member of the family, and the first to settle down.

He married Columba Garnica in 1974, when she was nineteen and he was twenty-one, and both were still in college. There was no parental objection to the marriage; George and Barbara had taken their vows at almost the same ages.

When Jeb announced he would run for governor of Florida in 1994, the decision surprised no one. He had already served as secretary of state.

Then George declared his intention to challenge Ann Richards in Texas, and even his mother tried to dissuade him. Ann had been a popular governor, a darling of the state and national media. When Barbara told her oldest son that his chances were not as good as Jeb's, he retorted, "Jeb might win. I *will* win."

When the returns came in on election night, Jeb had lost to the incumbent, Lawton Chiles. George W. had pulled off a startling upset, winning with 54 percent of the vote. When his parents called from Houston to tell the new governor of Texas how proud they were, he knew their enthusiasm was not unbridled. The hurt they felt for Jeb kept them from having total euphoria over his win. He could sense it in their voices, and he understood. But Jeb's turn would come. And in the year 2000, his state, Florida, won George W. the electoral votes to become the forty-third president and end the longest and zaniest election in at least a century.

11

---∽∞∽---

For All Things a Season

$\mathcal{I}$f ever a decision could be described as bittersweet, the one Prescott Bush made in the spring of 1962 qualified.

He had announced his plans to run for reelection to a third term a year earlier. He had reactivated the Bush for Senator Committee, organized a small campaign staff, raised money, filmed a television ad, and begun once again a grueling schedule of stumping Connecticut.

"One of the great burdens of the Senate," he would say later, "is this business of traveling around the state, and back and forth from Washington. This is exhausting when you are young, and in your upper sixties it becomes even more so. I was affected by that too strongly, I think.

"I was the only Republican from Connecticut to hold office in Congress in my last two years, and this meant that practically every event in the state demanded my presence. And being a loyal party man, I felt a responsibility to do all that I could. I would go back on a Friday and spend three days touring the state, from one event to another, then return to Washington on Monday, exhausted."

He had succumbed to a feeling shared by many politicians. They are like the aging Dalmatian, still excited by hearing the bells, still tempted by the chase, but left behind by the fire truck. He still maintained a heavy schedule in the Senate, had been troubled by arthritis, and pushing himself hard, had lost ten pounds. His tailored suits seemed to hang on him.

Any day is a good day for a foursome in George Bush's more leisurely life.

"So in that frame of mind," he said, "in the middle of May 1962, it seemed not too hard to convince myself that I didn't think I could carry on with the same vigor and enthusiasm. And perhaps some younger fellow deserved a chance at the job. I said to myself, 'What the hell? I'll be sixty-eight years old at the end of this term. I don't believe I can serve out another, with the pressures and strains of the office, given the state of health I was in.'"

Prescott had been to the hospital at Bethesda several times about his arthritis, but the doctors could do nothing for him. He went to his family physician in Greenwich for a checkup, and she told him flatly, "You would be a fool to run."

When Dorothy said she agreed with his doctor, the decision was made. Prescott Bush announced he would not run for reelection, and ripples of shock ran through both political parties in Connecticut.

"That was the whole story," he said. "In retrospect, I made the decision without adequate thought or deliberation. I wish I had checked into a hospital for four or five days or a week of rest. I often wish my doctor had said to me, 'Don't make a decision now. You're in the wrong state of mind.' But what she said was, 'You would be a fool to run.' I remember her language.

"I was in a state of exhaustion, and frankly, that is a poor time to be making an important decision. All the information we had at the time was favorable. The Democrats were having quite a fight within their party, and the public opinion polls showed that I would probably beat anybody they could put up.

"So looking back, not having been happy in retirement for nearly four years, and watching the political scene with interest, I do regret it. I think it was a disappointment to the people in my party and to many around the state. I probably would have survived another term just fine, if I had behaved myself and cut back a bit.

"Regrets weigh heavy on the mind. My health is good now because I have not had any strain or stress. The only stress I'm under is from inactivity. Once you have had the exposure to politics that I had—and I was a late bloomer at fifty-five—it gets in your blood. Then when you get out, nothing else satisfies that [excitement] in your blood. There is no substitute. It's like the old song, 'How are you going to keep him down on the farm, after he has seen Paree?'

"And that's true. I know so many who have been miserable after they left office. I saw Senator Keating of New York on the street, while he was in private law practice and before he became a judge on the state's high court. I said, 'Well, Ken, how are you liking it?'

"He said, 'For the first time in my life, I am making some money, as a lawyer. I have a beautiful office down here in the Pan Am Building and wonderful clients, and it's just great.'

"I said, 'Well, would you trade it for your Senate seat?'

"He said, 'Absolutely.' He said he would ten times rather be back in the Senate. I think most senators have that feeling. It's a very interesting, vital experience—very exciting. I do some banking business, but I was away from that for too long.

"I had been a managing partner of a big firm, and after I came back at sixty-eight, [I found that] this was too old to pick up a position like that. Those jobs were filled, and properly so. I didn't want to assume any real responsibilities there, and it would have been a terrible mistake if I had tried. They did want me to come back and make my offices there. From time to time, the partners will call on me for special duties. But I've lost the zest for banking, or any business, because I have been absorbed in matters that I found were much more satisfying, much more interesting, much more useful, and in all respects, better adapted to my temperament then going back into the business world."

These are strong sentiments for a man who once moved in financial circles open to only a privileged few, capable of cutting the deals of a lifetime. But his banking instincts were not entirely lost, even late in his life.

His son George came to visit him a few days before his death on October 9, 1972. The lung cancer that had been diagnosed only that summer had spread with alarming swiftness. The family had noticed a persistent cough, but he had felt well enough to play golf with his oldest son, Prescott Jr., a few days before he checked into Sloan-Kettering Memorial Hospital.

George Bush was then America's ambassador to the United Nations, and his office was only a few blocks from where his father was resting, heavily sedated. At least once a day he paid him a visit, talking to him about whatever he had been doing, not knowing if the dying man would be able to respond or not.

"He was in a bad way," said George, "just hanging on. I told him I had just come from having lunch that day with Andrei Gromyko, the Russian foreign minister. And to my surprise, Dad rallied a little and tried to raise himself up.

"He said, 'Who picked up the check?'"

In the end, he was thinking like a banker, but a senator as well, concerned no doubt for the hit the U.S. budget might have taken. For all his life, Prescott Bush had done his duty, with honor, and in his final days, had a whimsical thought for his son and their country.

And his legacy would live on.

Epilogue

The scent of oil had brought the Bush family to Texas in the first place, right after the end of World War II. Now the same fumes were bringing George W. back to Midland, where his roots had always been. Another oil boom was in the air, and this was a magnet for the risk takers, the gamblers, and the prophets who were on more than a treasure hunt.

Unlike gold or a hot stock, oil has been essential to human progress. It gave us the liquid fuel age, powered our cars and ships and planes, and enabled us to transport our dreams from one place to another. This pursuit of the earth's riches brings out the maverick and explorer in each of us.

After he received his masters from the Harvard Business School in 1975, George W. loaded his blue 1970 Cutlass and started driving west toward Texas. He did not have a fixed idea of what he wanted to do, but by the time he reached Midland he knew: He had decided to leap into the oil business.

Much has been made of the fact that he virtually retraced the trail his father had driven thirty years ago.

"I was not trying to follow in his footsteps," he insisted. "This was for me. The oil industry was, and is, completely result-oriented, just as sports and politics are."

He had no training and no firsthand knowledge about drilling for oil, except for one summer when he worked as a roughneck in the Louisiana oil fields. But as he grew up in Midland, the excitement and story-telling were all around him.

The return to Midland served as therapy for him. It was a refreshing change from the eastern snobbishness and the liberal bent of the campuses. He loved the casual lifestyle, the rough edges, and the hard honesty of men who had been flush and then broke and didn't let the cycle change them.

Young George rented a garage apartment and started out as a land man, working for independent producers at one hundred dollars a day. The job of a land man was to haunt the courthouses, searching through deeds to find out who owned the mineral rights to various pieces of property. Old-timers cherish the stories of the land men who bribed the operator in the telephone office, holding a line if they needed to report to their companies or raise more money while the less resourceful waited for hours.

Meanwhile George W. acquired some leases and formed an exploration business called Arbusto—Spanish for bush. His first few wells were dry holes, but he took comfort in the legends of the oil patch. One of the state's best known wildcatters, D. H. Byrd, had failed to bring in a well in seventy-two tries—a losing streak that led to his being called "Dry Hole Byrd" for the rest of his life. But once he began to hit, he knocked them down like bowling pins.

What young George needed was a company-maker, what the old

hands called "bagging the elephant." He ached to see that geyser of oil, hear that Niagara of noise, when the well is spouting beyond the derrick. In five years, his company drilled ninety-five wells, and hit oil or gas on roughly half of them, but the great gusher still eluded him. In 1982 he raised more than $2 million and changed the name of the company to Bush Exploration. Two years later he merged Bush Exploration with a drilling company called Spectrum 7, co-owned by two of his friends, Bill DeWitt and Mercer Reynolds.

Oil prices had gone down the drain in the early 1980s. By the spring of 1986, the price per barrel had dropped from twenty-nine dollars to nine. The prevailing mood was captured by a story that made the rounds.

Two well-dressed matrons were walking in downtown Midland, when a frog jumped in front of them and said, "I'm not really a frog, I'm a Texas oilman. An evil witch cast a spell on me, and if a pretty woman would give me a kiss I will change back."

One of the ladies reached down, picked up the frog, opened her purse, dropped him in, and snapped the purse shut.

Her companion said, "Aren't you going to give him a kiss?"

The first woman replied, "Hell, no. A talking frog is worth a helluva lot more than a Texas oilman."

With oil prices near the bottom, Spectrum 7 couldn't afford to drill new wells. George W. began to look for a public company to acquire Spectrum 7, giving its investors a chance to recover some of their money through stock. That goal led him to Harken Energy, based in Irving, Texas, where the Dallas Cowboys had their complex. They were able to swap the assets of Spectrum 7 for liquidity, in the form of publicly traded stock in Harken worth $2 million.

In June 1990 George W. sold some 200,000 shares for $848,560, before taxes. In late August Harken reported a serious second quarter loss. Government regulators reviewed the sale, and no wrongdoing was found.

Other questions were raised about a contract Harken won to explore for oil off the coast of Bahrain, an emirate in the Persian Gulf. Some were quick to conclude that Harken received this concession based on George W.'s relationship with the man in the White House. But the directors of the company insisted that George W. opposed the deal. He doubted that any significant oil would be found and was wary of the instability in that part of the world. As it turned out, Harken came up empty.

No one knew where the bottom was, either. Independent oilmen were shutting down all around him. It was time for George W. to declare victory and take on another challenge. Oil, politics, and baseball have always been a part of George W. Now that he had done the "oil" thing, George W. was off to Washington to help his father campaign for president. Although he loved politics, baseball was part of his heritage, too, and George W. had yet to bag his "elephant."

One if the proudest moments of his life, he had said, was the day his father no longer had to hold back on his throws. The boy who had filled a shoe box with cards of players both great and forgettable would, as a part owner, expand his collection of autographed balls to 150, each in a plastic bubble. While George W. was in Washington working on his father's campaign, former Yale classmate Bill DeWitt called one day to say that the Texas Rangers were for sale.

"Hey, here's our chance," he said. "We can buy the Rangers. You want to get back to Texas, and this could be a natural."

Over Christmas George W. called Rangers owner Eddie Chiles and told him he would like to make an offer on the club.

Eddie replied, "You don't have any money."

George W. said, "That's right, but we're putting a group together."

Putting the group together became his mission. He stayed in touch with Chiles and his lawyers and lined up a group of friends willing to go in on the deal. The group included Roland Betts, who demanded—and received—a promise from him not to run for political office in 1990.

"I'm not going to put in a bunch of money," he said, direct as ever, "if you're not going to be there." Like his grandfather before him, when faced with the political itch amidst business responsibilities, George W. restrained his desires and remained loyal to his duties.

Politics was in the blood of George W. Bush, though, and a run for governor—a fairly brash thought—had been on his mind. But acquiring the Rangers and building a badly needed new stadium quickly became his obsession. He needed that sense of accomplishment, especially in a venture that had meaning for the state of Texas. That would meet his obligation to the family code established by Prescott Bush: "Before you enter public service, you go out and make some money and take care of your family." But more than that, Prescott had believed that, if you had money, it came with an obligation to serve.

The purchase price for the Rangers was $86 million, and he told Laura that he was going to be like a pit bull, grab a pants leg and not let go until the deal was done. The proceeds from his earlier sale of Harken stock would provide the cash he needed to pay for his interest in the team. When the deal was made, he put in $606,000, almost all of his cash and a third of his net worth.

The ownership group George W. put together included Craig Stapleton, a Connecticut real estate developer and a cousin by marriage; Fred Malek, who had been an adviser to President Nixon; Richard Rainwater, an investment manager whose clients included the Bass brothers; and Edward "Rusty" Rose, known to his friends as the "mortician."

The rarest of sights: President Bush with four living ex-presidents: (left to right) Gerald Ford, Richard Nixon, Ronald Reagan, and Jimmy Carter in the Oval Office.

George W. took an office at the ballpark, while Rose, who disliked giving speeches, stayed at his corporate offices in Dallas. George W. did like making speeches, so he traveled around the area and across the state, selling the ball club. He would mix in a reference or two to his mother and father, connect baseball to patriotism, and stress how reasonable the ticket prices were and the family-friendly nature of the game.

The Rangers' new ownership inherited a franchise that had never had a winning season in twenty-five years. Moreover, their history with managers was wretched. The low point was in June 1977 when there were four managers in one week. Then-owner Brad Corbett fired Frank Lucchesi, replacing him with Eddie Stanky, the old Dodgers spark plug who had been coaching college ball in Alabama. Stanky managed the team to a 10–8 win over the Minnesota Twins, had a change of heart the next morning, and before dawn caught a plane back to Mobile. One of the coaches, Connie Ryan, became the interim manager, until Billy Hunter was hired to be the team's fourth skipper in six days.

By comparison, under the Bush group the club became stable and consistent. Bobby Valentine was in his fifth year as manager, and starting in 1989, he'd finish with eighty-three or more victories in the next three seasons.

George W. got to know the ushers, grounds crew, and office staff by name, and quite a few of the fans, "some of whom I would see at all eighty-one games. It was like a small family. You just have to understand, the baseball fan owns the team, too."

George W. signed hundreds of autographs, mostly for kids who wanted one from Nolan Ryan but would settle for the son of a president who also happened to be one of the owners of the club.

He made it a point not to sit in the owners' box or the press box but always to take a front row seat next to the dugout. That was part of his job, as he saw it, sitting among the fans. This meant, of course, that he sometimes heard the heckling: "Bush, hey, Bush, more pitching." For him, however, this didn't seem much different from what he had seen in politics. You just had to develop a thick skin and a rational way to defend your decisions.

One night a leather-lunged fan a few rows behind him kept yelling his name. He turned around, spotted the source, and introduced himself. The heckler was a teacher at a local high school.

"Do you like having your name yelled out in public?" George W. asked. The man said no. "Neither do I," retorted Bush. "Let's talk about it."

They had an interesting conversation. The teacher apologized for yelling at him, and George W. apologized for the pitching.

A few years later, after he had been elected to his first term as governor, this same fan showed up at a Rangers game when George W. happened to be in the crowd. The fan rushed up to an usher and said, "I have to see Governor Bush." It turned out he just wanted to know how George W. was doing since his career change. They had become ballpark buddies.

The partners built value in the franchise in two ways. They kept the payroll within reasonable limits and never lost money. The second reason was the new stadium, part of the original vision. Going to Rangers games became fashionable.

The voters of Arlington passed a bond issue, by a wide margin, to approve a half-cent sales tax that would finance the stadium's first $135 million, with the Rangers putting up the rest and paying an annual rent.

The Ballpark at Arlington opened in April 1994. It was a model partnership. If all went according to plan, the bonds would be paid off ahead of time and the tax would be dropped.

And they kept the team in Texas, not a sure thing without a new park.

For George and Laura, it was the best time of their lives, enjoying the pace of the game, sitting with friends and sometimes with his twin daughters. Little Barbara commented one night on the fireflies in the park. And on some of those long nights when the Rangers were out of the game early, Laura and George were able to spend two or three hours of quality time, just talking.

"Take Me Out to the Ball Game" is not just a song, it's an anthem. George, Bar, Laura, and George W. at the new Ballpark at Arlington.

On one memorable occasion, the family celebrated the five thousandth strikeout by Nolan Ryan, then one of the Rangers. It was a special night, dubbed "Texas Heat One," with Ryan facing off against Roger Clemens of the Red Sox. The Rangers' Rafael Palmiero hit a two-run homer, and Jeff Russell saved it in the ninth, for a memorable win.

In July 1999 when Ryan was voted into the Hall of Fame at

Cooperstown, he said of George W., then in his second term as governor, "We had a unique relationship. I only planned on pitching one season, and I stayed for five, and he paid me a whole lot of money. Now I'm working for him again on the Parks and Wildlife Commission, and he doesn't pay me anything."

Reporters frequently asked George W. if baseball and politics are in any way similar. "Absolutely," he said, quoting Joe Garagiola, the announcer and former catcher: "Baseball gives you every chance to be great. Then it puts every pressure on you to prove that you haven't got what it takes. It never takes away that chance, and it never takes away that pressure." That description applies just as well to politics.

In both the message matters. In baseball it's "We want your family." In politics it's "This is what I believe." The message has to be simple and consistent. *We know you have other options. We hope you will give us a look.*

In 1994, with the completion of the new stadium and with the franchise being well established, George W. was freed from his obligations. One of the partners, Tom Schieffer, a lawyer and former state representative, was given both the role of president and overseer of the new, retro ballpark. George W. resigned, to the surprise of many and against the advice of his own mother, to run for governor. When Bush upset the incumbent, Ann Richards, he did so by tailoring his message to four primary issues, by stressing his Midland and west Texas roots, and with a twang at least as cozy as hers.

Richards tried to make mileage out of his business history during the governor's race, but that tactic backfired. Too many people across the state had been bruised by the fallout from the oil industry's decline.

George W. had drawn an important lesson from his father's experience, however: Family values strike a significant chord in the heart of America.

After he was elected governor of Texas in 1994, this was brought home to him on an occasion when he, Laura, and the twins were on a series of nature hikes around the state, promoting Texas tourism. Their first stop was at Quanah, where Laura Bush endorsed a project to revitalize Main Street.

After the governor spoke in the town square, a man squeezed his way through the crowd to shake his hand. While the girls looked on, the man said, "Son, it was right here on this spot thirty years ago that I heard your daddy give a speech when he was running against Ralph Yarborough."

During his first campaign for governor, the media was eager for George W.'s reaction when Ross Perot endorsed Anne Richards two weeks before the election. (He always believed—still believes—that Perot's third-party candidacy cost his father the White House in 1996.)

He didn't have to issue a prepared statement. His response was, "That's all right. She can have Ross Perot, and I'll take Nolan Ryan."

If praise was currency, Ryan was always well compensated. "Nolan meant a lot to the Rangers," said Bush, "not only because of his milestone games: the three hundredth win, the two no-hitters, the five thousandth strikeout. He was a hero who didn't let us down, a public figure who didn't betray the trust. He was and is a true Texan, with a beautiful family."

Ryan, defying the calendar with every start, pumped new life into the franchise, after twenty years with the Mets, Angels and Astros, drawing big crowds and delivering big performances, right up to his final start in September 1993, at Seattle. On that occasion, he felt a pop in his right elbow on his last pitch and walked off the field, his arm limp at his side, waving his cap to the crowd with his left hand.

In 1998 George W. had been running the state for four years. At that time he and the group sold the Rangers to Tom Hicks for $250 million. George W.'s cut, with bonus, was $14 million. He finally bagged his elephant and was now able to focus entirely on politics, setting his sights higher than Texas.

And the legacy continued.

There is no neat or easy transition from the batter's box to the voter's booth, except for the part about losing. Baseball teaches you not to accept or tolerate defeat but to keep it in perspective: You start over every day.

The language of the sport found its way into the other medium, of course. *Playing hardball, team player,* and on occasion, *caught stealing* are among the common phrases.

More than any other game, baseball is a game of absolutes, and this had been part of the appeal to Prescott, to Poppy and George W., to all the Bush and Walker men. Polls were not needed. The media kept score but had no power to change it. If the umpire called you out on strike three, not even Johnnie Cochran could get you off.

In November 1992 the presidency of George Herbert Walker Bush was in its last inning. Almost to the very end he believed the American people would move away from Bill Clinton and the unpredictable Ross Perot, whose third man theme had so muddled the race. The voters would remember and reward his leadership. He had dispatched American troops to arrest the Panamanian dictator and drug

George and Barbara Bush leave the White House in January 1993 as their staffs and well-wishers look on. They celebrated their 57th wedding anniversary in 2002; the longest marriage of any U.S. president.

trafficker Manuel Noriega. He had organized the coalition that won the Gulf War and made Saddam Hussein a prisoner in his own country. On his watch the Soviet Union had collapsed and the forces of western democracy had won the Cold War.

But Americans have a notoriously short attention span. Nor had they noticed that the economy, in the tank for two years, had begun to rally in the last quarter. Clinton and Al Gore won by a margin of 43 percent to 38 percent, with Perot, in and out and back in the campaign, taking 19 percent, which under the circumstances was a surprising figure. No one really knew how the vendetta had started, but few in the Bush inner circle doubted that the Dallas billionaire had thrown the election to the Democrats.

In the final week of the campaign, President Bush located a favorite photograph of his father released by the U. S. Golf Association the year Prescott became its president, in 1935. He had his office mail it to his oldest son. A copy of the note he sent with it is in the archives of the George Bush Presidential Library on the campus at Texas A&M. "Dear George," the note said, "Someone gave me this shot of Dad, and I thought you might like to have for your scrapbook."

The night before the election, as Air Force One flew toward Texas, the Oak Ridge Boys, who

The U.S.G.A. released this official photograph of Prescott in 1935, the year he became its president.

had appeared with the president at various campaign stops, swung out a medley of gospel songs. Bill Minutaglio, who wrote the first George W. biography, described a tender and touching vignette aboard the plane: "And when they started singing the ultimate going-to-the-hereafter anthem, 'Amazing Grace,' George W. and his father began to sing along. The two were in tears, and his father said the song had made him think about *his* father—about Prescott Bush."

You lose and the next day you started over, except this time a new generation would have its turn. In 1994 George W. and Jeb would be candidates for governor in Texas and Florida. A chorus line of Bush ladies, Barbara and Laura and Columba, expressed virtually the same thought: "For the first time, the sons were out of the shadow of their father. They were on their own. They were liberated."

Running a disciplined and tightly controlled race, George W.

pulled off the stunning upset of the popular incumbent, Ann Richards. The two of them had attracted national interest, especially so among both political parties. Overnight, the first son had been propelled into the limelight as a potential presidential contender.

Jeb Bush had lost by just under seventy-five thousand votes to Florida's incumbent governor, Lawton Chiles. Seven years younger, Jeb did not feel the pressures or the comparisons that dogged his older brother, the president's namesake. He had settled in Florida in a conscious attempt to avoid the same fate. Taller than his dad, he favored the Pierces, Barbara's side of the family. His face is baby soft and expressive, and at times takes on the beatific look of his mother.

This election night was when the former President uttered the poignant line about his sons, "The joy is in Texas, but our hearts are in Florida."

On the eve of the elections in 1998, George Herbert Walker Bush took a sheet of stationary and wrote of the feelings that were nearly overwhelming:

Tomorrow I might well be the dad of the governors of the second and fourth largest states in the Union. But there will be no feelings of personal vindication, no feeling of anything other than pride in two honest boys who, for the right reasons, want to serve—who fought the good fight and won.

And so they did. Jeb had learned from his defeat and adopted his brother's strategy. He streamlined his campaign, as George W. had done, reducing his issues to four: education, juvenile justice, tort, and welfare reforms. Jeb also decided to be more outgoing and less

After being sworn in Governor George W. Bush listens to his democratic ally,
Lieutenant Governor Bob Bullock, as he often did.

wonkish. The makeover worked. He won in double digits over the
Democrat, Ken McKay, the lieutenant governor. George W. was
being reelected in Texas, with some 70 percent of the vote, against
Garry Mauro, a protégé of his Democratic ally, Bob Bullock.

The courting of Bullock, a crusty, crafty, recovering alcoholic, five
times married, was the key to George W.'s successful term and a half.
As lieutenant governor, Bullock had the power to whip bills through
the legislature. The younger George sought him out, asked for his
advice, deferred to his judgment. Bullock, who was the godfather to
Mauro's daughter, wound up supporting Bush.

A parade of prominent Republicans began flying into Austin to
stage what amounted to a virtual draft of George W. for the 2000
presidential nomination. Even as he pondered whether or not to run,
he established a blue ribbon committee to be the caretaker for the

millions in campaign contributions that were already being made.

He had the backing of the party's hard core conservative wing and the Christian Coalition, constituencies that had never fully embraced his father. He was ready for the sin and lifestyle questions that had become part of the process—about his drinking, drugs, his frat boy mischief, his National Guard service. He deflected most of the questions with one nimble line: "When I was young and irresponsible, I was young and irresponsible."

The politics of destruction had moved into another gear. In Prescott's time, the media was hesitant to ask about his golf score.

There were shaky moments in the early weeks of the campaign as George W. found his voice, forged a kind of truce with the media hounds, and sharpened his message and his style. He weathered an unexpectedly tough challenge from John McCain, the Arizona senator and former prisoner of war in Vietnam. A victory in the South Carolina primary would be the campaign's turning point.

He selected Dick Cheney, his father's former secretary of defense, as his running mate and accepted his party's nomination at a convention that included seventy-five of his relatives. One of them was Jeb's

Another father and son duo hit the national stage: Governor Jeb Bush of Florida and his son George Prescott Bush.

son, George Prescott Bush: handsome, athletic, fluent in Spanish, then a student at the University of Texas, and perhaps the family's political star of the future.

George W. Bush and Dick Cheney squared off against Al Gore and Joe Lieberman, the senator from Connecticut who happened to occupy the seat once held by Prescott Bush. In what would become the strangest election in roughly one hundred years, the contest came down to a recount of ballots cast in the state governed by Jeb Bush. The television networks first called Florida for Al Gore, then pulled it back and called it for George W. Bush. And in the wee hours of the morning, the state was dropped into the category of "too close to call."

Something called a butterfly ballot had confused a few thousand voters in Dade County, and the numbers were in conflict in at least three others. The country became familiar with the terms "hanging chads" and "dimpled ballots." So the campaign did not end on election night, or even four weeks later. In the first week in December 2000, Florida's secretary of state, Katherine Harris, certified George W. as the winner by 537 votes. In short order, the Florida Supreme Court ruled on a Friday that the recount could continue but had to be completed by 6:00 P.M. on Sunday.

Gore had won the popular vote by a margin that would reach five hundred thousand, but the electoral votes in Florida would put Bush over the top. As anger and confusion and frustration swept and divided the country, the controversy went to the Supreme Court, which ended the recount and by a 5-4 vote accepted the recount certified by the office of Katherine Harris.

George W. Bush had become the 43rd President of the United

States, moving into the White House eight years after his father had left. He took with him his Texas issues and a promise to unify the country and cut taxes. Wall Street and the business world welcomed his inauguration as the first president to manage the government as a CEO. This label would be shed in the aftermath of two turbulent events that changed the way Americans lived and hoped.

George W.'s grandfather, Prescott Bush, had stepped off the Yale campus and into a field artillery captain's uniform to serve in France during the First World War. His father enlisted right out of prep school in the Navy Air Force to fight for his country in the Pacific. George W.'s war came to him, and to America, in a terrorist attack that cost nearly three thousand civilian lives. It horrified and devastated the nation.

On September 11, 2001, nineteen hijackers turned three out of four commercial airliners into flying bombs and struck at the symbols of American might and security. These hideous attacks leveled the World Trade Center Towers, destroyed part of the Pentagon, and left us in a mood not unlike what the country experienced after Japanese planes wiped out much of the U. S. fleet at Pearl Harbor.

As his father eight years before him, George W. Bush takes the oath of office from Chief Justice Rehnquist.

213

There is no point, really, in comparing the depths of our pain or the dimensions of our national tragedies. The suicide flights that caused the Twin Towers to collapse stabbed at the soul of New York, the spirit of America, and our way of life. But it was not another Pearl Harbor.

Those who died on December 7, 1941, were mostly in the military. Given the nature of a surprise attack that came just after dawn, they were able to mount a defense, racing to their anti-aircraft guns and launching fighter planes that were not in flames on the ground.

The victims this time were overwhelmingly civilians. This was the slaughter of the innocents, a death toll that would not be accurately calculated for a year. Only one fact was undisputed. As Mayor Rudolph Guliani put it, "When we have the final number, it will be more than we can bear." We weighed the broken hearts and measured the trail of tears for weeks and months, and America learned that mourning does not get easier with practice.

The hijackers were identified as members of the terrorist organization, al-Qaida, headed by Osama bin Laden, who left Saudi Arabia as a rich man and used his wealth to finance a worldwide network of terror. The ruling political and religious party in Afghanistan, The Taliban, had given bin Laden and his murderers shelter and support.

The president ordered American planes and troops into action, bombing Taliban bases in Afghanistan and hunting down the assassins of al-Qaida. He announced the formation of a Homeland Security Agency and put into effect a series of new security measures. What emerged from the American response was a doctrine that called for the use of American force anywhere in the world to counter and eliminate the purveyors of terror. The idea of a corporate president evaporated. George W. emerged as the country's commander in chief, and he expressed thoughts and spoke words that reassured a troubled and grieving population. Any question of his legitimacy as president had been answered.

We may never come to terms with the number of deaths. The image of people at work, at their desks—bankers and stock brokers, secretaries and clerks—are not easily forgotten. The sight of two planes plowing into the towers, looking so much like Hollywood special effects, has been seared into our brains.

The reality of 9-11 was ghastly, unthinkable, maddening. The New York skyline was altered forever. Life as we knew it may never return to normal. But George W. Bush offered leadership as the country rallied and renewed itself.

Then, with his approval ratings topping out in the high eighties and still holding at nearly 70 percent, the president took a gamble, a big and bold one. He used his political capital to campaign extensively in fifteen states for Republican candidates, in an effort to gain a majority for his party in the Senate and strengthen their grip in Congress. And he succeeded beyond anyone's expectations, including in Florida, where Jeb Bush won reelection in a landslide. That night, the 41st president was in Talahassee to re-introduce his son, shouting into a microphone to be heard over the buzz in the auditorium: "It gives me great pride to introduce your current and next governor, Jeb Bush."

His older brother made at least ten trips to the state, raising millions and rallying the Republican base. Asked if the president was playing favorites, Jeb quipped, "He has been helping me more than Bill Clinton did during my first two years in office. Why? He loves Florida. He loves me, too, and I love him."

The Bushes have had a broad and indelible impact on American politics. Although there appears to be one, the family is ambivalent towards the notion of a dynasty. Jeb expressed the sentiment well when he said that "it connotes something that has been kind of given to you, and it hasn't been. We have worked very hard to get to a point where we can serve people. We learned to overcome the fears and trepidation of politics from our grandfather and our father. But I wouldn't call it a dynasty. I think everybody kind of cringes when we hear the word."

In the week after his sweeping re-election, Jeb reflected on the tribal commitment and the man who set it in motion: "I remember when I was visiting him in his later years. We were having dinner and he said, 'Don't call me Gampy. That makes me sound too old. Call me Senator.' Then he tells my Ganny, 'Dorothy, I always appreciate it when our grandkids come to eat with us, since we always eat better.'

"He was a stern man until his later years. But he was full of character. It oozed out of him. He was the standard for what was right and fair. When he died, my Dad replaced him and raised the bar, in my humble opinion.

"I learned from my Dad, who learned from his Dad, about integrity. Doing what you think is right is a lot more important than being popular. Principles matter a lot more than public opinion polls."

Starting in Connecticut, spreading its wings to Texas and Florida, the legacy lives on.

Bibliography

The bulk of the material for this book was developed from forty-six hours of taped interviews with members of the Bush family and friends as well as from the Prescott Bush Oral History Project. The Project took place in 1966, and the tapes and transcripts have been entrusted to the George Bush Presidential Library on the campus of Texas A&M University and the archives and special collections of the Thomas Dodd Research Center, University of Connecticut. Portions of the Prescott Bush interviews, and a family scrapbook, were available for the first time for this undertaking. Every Bush biographer expresses his or her respect for the exhaustive research of Herbert S. Parmet in his 1996 biography of the elder George Bush, *A Lone Star Yankee*. We gratefully add ours to that list.

Other sources include:

BOOKS

Bush, Barbara. *Barbara Bush: A Memoir*." New York: Scribner's, 1994.

Bush, George. *All the Best, My Life in Letters and Other Writings*. New York: Lisa Drew/Scribner, 1999.

Bush, George W. *A Charge to Keep*. New York: HarperCollins, 1999.

Bush, George and Victor Gold. *Looking Forward*. New York: Bantam, 1988.

Cramer, Richard Ben. *What It Takes*. New York: Random House, 1992. A reference to the youthful appearance of George Bush in the opening paragraph of chapter one is a variation of a description that appears on page 80 of *What It Takes* and also a topic of family teasing.

Minutaglio, Bill. *First Son*. New York: Times Books, 1999.

Mitchell, Elizabeth. *W — "Revenge of the Bush Dynasty*. New York: Hyperion, 2000.

Parmet, Herbert S. *George Bush, The Life of a Lone Star Yankee*. New York: Lisa Drew/Scribner, 1996.

Radcliffe, Donnie. *Simply Barbara Bush*. New York: Warner Books, 1989.

ARTICLES

Alexander, Paul, "All Hat, No Cattle," *Rolling Stone* (August 1999).

Birnbaum, Jeffrey H., "The Man Who Could be President," *Fortune* (March 1999).

Burka, Paul, "The W. Nobody Knows," *Texas Monthly* (June 1999). From the series, *Who Is George W. Bush?*

Burkeman, Oliver, "The Tomb Raiders," *Guardian* (London), April 2000.

Colloff, Pamela, "The Son Rises," *Texas Monthly* (June 1999). From the series, *Who Is George W. Bush?*

Feldman, Trude B., "Dorothy Bush: Moral Leader for a Family," *Fresno Bee* (June 1991).

———, "Ganny Bush at 90," *San Francisco Examiner* (June 1991).

Hart, Patricia Kilday, "Not So Great in '78," *Texas Monthly* (June 1999). From the series, *Who Is George W. Bush?*

Hollandsworth, Skip, "Born to Run: What's in a Name?" *Texas Monthly* (May 1994).

———, "Younger, Wilder?" *Texas Monthly* (June 1999). From the series, *Who Is George W. Bush?*

Kranish, Michael, "An American Dynasty," parts 1 and 2, *Boston Globe* (July 2001).

Noah, Timothy, "Old Bland-Dad, Meet Poppy's Poppa," *The New Republic* (April 1989).

Patoski, Joe Nick, "Team Player," *Texas Monthly* (June 1999). From the series, *Who Is George W. Bush?*

Robbins, Alexandra, "George W., Knight of Eulogia," *Atlantic Monthly* (May 2000).

Smith, Evan, "George, Washington," *Texas Monthly* (June 1999). From the series, *Who Is George W. Bush?*

Sullivan, Andrew, "Counter Culture: All in the Family," *The New York Times Sunday Magazine* (September 2000).

Thorpe, Helen, "Go East, Young Man," *Texas Monthly* (June 1999). From the series, *Who Is George W. Bush?*

Index

The italicized numbers indicate photographs. Due to the large number of occurrences only the photographs for George Herbert Walker Bush, George Walker Bush, and Prescott Bush are indexed.